word and music games

for toddlers and twos

Dr Bonnie Macmillan

hamlyn

First published in Great Britain in
2004 by Hamlyn, a division of
Octopus Publishing Group Limited,
2–4 Heron Quays,
London E14 4JP

Copyright © 2004 Octopus Publishing
Group Limited

Distributed in the United States
and Canada by
Sterling Publishing Co., Inc.
387 Park Avenue South, New York,
NY 10016-8810

ISBN 0 600 60994 4

A CIP catalogue record for this book
is available from the British Library

Printed and bound in China

10 9 8 7 6 5 4 3 2 1

contents

introduction

Normal, loving and responsive care-giving is fundamental to helping your child fulfil her intellectual potential. Once this is in place, however, one form of stimulation that has been proven to make a real difference is language.

You can raise your child's IQ simply by engaging her in lots of conversation, encouraging her responses and enjoying each other's company. Because language is the main avenue to learning about the world, it is likely that just talking and listening to your child is the most important form of intellectual stimulation she will ever receive.

Music is another form of stimulation that has been shown to boost brain development. The processing of musical sounds is closely related to the processing of speech sounds: both activate similar brain regions, suggesting that music is a sort of pre-linguistic language. The ability to listen is a prerequisite to analysing both speech and musical sounds.

The language, music and listening games in this book are primarily for fun. It is not the intention to 'push' or pressurize your child, but simply to enhance her development through shared activities that are enjoyable for both of you.

Language

Between the ages of 7 and 12 months, the sound of a baby's babbling begins to change subtly. More consonant sounds creep in, and by 12 months a baby may speak her first word – a thrilling moment for every parent. Although the age at which this happens is not related to subsequent language development, a child's vocabulary at 3 years does predict vocabulary as an adult.

Research shows that during the first 3 years, when brain growth is at its peak, parents can make a tremendous difference to their child's

subsequent vocabulary and IQ. Three factors count: the quantity of language spoken directly to the child (not just overheard), the quality of language the child hears (number of descriptive words, less common words, word explanations), and the parents' style of interacting with the child (that is, how responsive, positive and encouraging they are).

Music

The main characteristics of music – pitch, timbre, intensity and rhythm – are all found in spoken language. For this reason, musical experience can help a child listen to, remember, integrate and produce language sounds. In the same way that a baby plays with speech sounds while babbling, repeated tunes, songs and nursery rhymes are seen as games by young children – as 'toys' for the ear and voice.

Apart from the effects of music on language development, exposing your child to musical activities or instruction can result in many other benefits including a higher IQ, enhanced abstract reasoning ability, improved auditory memory, increased creativity and better manual dexterity.

Listening

Skilled listening requires a child to concentrate on selected sounds. Listening ability is the starting point for a vast amount of learning, whether through exposure to language or to all kinds of music.

The talking, listening, rhyming, singing, reading, finger-play, music and movement games in this book are designed to help accelerate the 'wiring up' of language, music and listening circuits in the brain – all essential to the full realization of your child's intellectual potential.

all about me

games to help your child learn about body parts

bath action

A A

from 18 months

This game focuses on the names of body parts as well as some interesting action words (verbs).

- Make your toddler's bath toys perform and encourage her to tell you what each one is doing.

- Pick up the fish and say 'Oh look! The fish is diving, diving, diving under your leg! What is it doing?' Make it dive several times under your toddler's leg and see if she can tell you 'It is diving'.

- Then pick up the soap and say 'Oh look! The soap is washing, washing, washing your hands. What is it doing?'

- Continue with other objects, linking their actions with your child's body parts. For example: the boat is zooming, zooming, zooming past your tummy; the frog is splashing, splashing, splashing on your back, and so on.

RESEARCH SAYS...

'The repetition of words and phrases is one of the best ways to accelerate your child's language development. It helps to reinforce the neural pathways in her brain that link sound with meaning.'

bear, bee & tabby cat
from 2 years

Repeating favourite hand and finger games helps your child recognize familiar words and phrases.

- Ask your toddler to hold out her hand, palm upwards. Gently draw a circle round and round on her palm with your finger, saying 'Round and round the garden, like a teddy bear...'

- 'Walk' your fingers slowly up her arm, saying 'One step, two steps...' Then, as you say 'And tickle you under there!' tickle her under her arm.

- Now try: 'Round and round the garden, like a bumblebee... One flight, two flights (make your hand take two pouncing 'flights' up her arm)... And a tickle from me!'

- Go back to the original version, but substitute 'tabby cat' for 'teddy bear', and finish with 'And tickle you like that!'

in & out
from 2 years

Linking words with actions will help to extend vocabulary and concentration skills.

- Stand facing your child. Put your hand out in front of you, then behind, as you say 'Put this hand in, take this hand out, put this hand in, now shake it all about.' See if she can copy your actions and words.

- Now try: 'Put your fingers in your ears, pull your fingers out...', 'Put this leg in, take this leg out...', 'Put that arm in, take that arm out...'. Shake the body part each time.

- Later you can teach 'up' and 'down' and 'under' and 'over', matching your words with appropriate actions.

the toe family
from 18 months

- Sit your toddler on your lap, hold her big toe and ask 'What toe is this?' Pause, then say 'This is great big daddy toe. He can stretch!' Gently pull her toe.

- Move to the next toe, asking 'What toe is this?' Pause, then say 'This is mummy toe. She can bend!' Gently bend the toe.

- Continue with 'brother toe', saying 'He can throw and catch!' Bend this toe gently back and forth.

- Next comes 'sister toe' and 'She can giggle!' Shake this toe a little.

- Finish with 'baby toe', who 'likes to wiggle and jiggle all the way home!' Jiggle this toe, and tickle and bounce your child on your knee. With time, see if she can supply the name of each toe.

Playing this game will help your toddler learn the names of family members and some interesting actions.

two things at once
from 2 years

This game is an excellent way to boost your toddler's listening and verbal memory skills, while improving balance and co-ordination.

- Ask your toddler 'Can you touch your nose like this?' Put one finger on the end of your nose and see if she can copy you. Say 'Well done!' and keep your finger on your nose.

- Now say 'Can you touch your ear like this at the same time?' Move on to other double pointing actions: cheek and chin, tummy and neck, ankle and toe, and so on.

- Always give one instruction at a time. Make sure she can point to one body part before adding a second.

what are these for?

from 2 years

- Hold up both hands, asking 'What are these for? Hands are for folding.' (Fold hands together.) 'And for clapping – clap, clap!' (Clap twice.) Encourage your child to copy your words and actions.

- Show your toes, asking 'What are these for? Toes are for pointing.' (Point to toes.) 'And tapping – tap! tap!' (Tap toes twice.)

- Point to both eyes, asking 'What are these for? Eyes are for sleeping.' (Close eyes.) 'And looking – yes, boo!' (Open eyes wide.)

- Point to your nose, asking 'But what is this for? A nose is for sniffing.' (Sniff.) 'And sneezing – ah-choo!' (Pretend to sneeze.)

This action rhyme is a fun way to expand your child's vocabulary and teach her what certain body parts are useful for.

RESEARCH SAYS...

Between the ages of 1 and 3 years, the average number of words parents address directly to their children each hour varies from as little as 600 to more than 2,000. The more words children hear, the better their vocabulary and IQ scores.

chinny chin-chin

from 18 months

Alliteration appeals to children of this age. This game will draw your toddler's attention to various speech sounds and encourage her to try using them herself.

- Face your toddler, point to her chin and say 'Oh look! Here's your... (pause) ... chinny chin-chin!' Emphasize the 'ch' sound and rub your chins together.

- Ask 'What is it?' Pause, encouraging your child to answer with you: 'It's your... chinny chin-chin.'

- Now point to your child's cheek and say 'Oh look! Here's your cheeky cheek-cheek!' Rub cheeks together and ask 'What is it? It's your... cheeky cheek-cheek.'

- Continue with other body parts: lippy lip-lips, nosey nose-nose, handy hand-hand and so on.

RESEARCH SAYS...

The best way to enhance your toddler's language development is to have lots of one-on-one conversations, where you take turns listening and responding to each other.

my turn, your turn

from 18 months

Games where you and your toddler take turns, as in conversation, are an ideal way to boost her language abilities.

- Sit facing your child and say 'Look! Here's mummy's (daddy's) tummy!'

- Touch your stomach and ask 'Do you have a tummy? Where's your tummy?' Help your child to find, and point to, her tummy.

- Point to her tummy and ask (as if you've forgotten already) 'What's this again?' This gives your child a chance to name the body part herself.

- Continue in this way with other body parts.

where oh where?

from 18 months

Your toddler loves hiding games and this one is an excellent way to introduce her to the names of different body parts.

- Cover your head with a cloth and say 'Where oh where is mummy's (daddy's) *head*?', emphasizing the word 'head'. If your toddler doesn't immediately pull the cloth off, encourage her by shaking your head a little.

- Once she has found your head, exclaim 'Oh yes, here's my *head*!' as you point to it.

- Now cover other body parts and see if your toddler can find them.

fee fie foe opposites

from 2 years

- Begin with 'Fee fie foe fum, oh here it is, here's mummy's (daddy's) *great big* thumb!' Emphasize the adjectives 'great big' and hold up your thumb.

- Repeat this rhyme together so that your child has a chance to use these words herself.

- Now say 'Fee fie foe fum, where is (your child's name)'s *tiny little* thumb?' Emphasize the words 'tiny little'. Your child should now hold up her thumb for comparison. Then repeat the rhyme together.

- Once your toddler is familiar with the concepts of 'great big' and 'tiny little', introduce other opposites such as fat and thin, short and tall, large and small.

This game is similar to Fee Fie Foe Fum! (see opposite), but includes adjectives describing size. Children learn to use these later than many other adjectives.

finer fee fie foe

from 2 years

Expand your child's vocabulary and observational skills by focusing on the finer descriptive details of different people's body parts.

- Sit facing your toddler and say 'Fee fie foe fum, here's (your child's name)'s... dusty knee.' Use an appropriate adjective: grazed, bent, straight, chubby and so on.

- Repeat this rhyme together so that your child has a chance to use the new adjective.

- Now say 'Fee fie foe fum, here's mummy's (daddy's) knee. What does it look like?' Discuss its appearance in as much detail as possible.

- Continue with other body parts, helping your child to notice how the details differ for each of you.

fee fie foe fum!

from 2 years

- Sit in a comfortable position with your child. Say 'Fee fie foe *fum*, oh here it is, here's mummy's (daddy's) thumb!' Hold up your thumb for her to see.

- Now say 'Fee fie foe *fum*, oh here it is, here's (your child's name)'s thumb!' Hold up your child's thumb for display.

- Continue in this way for other body parts, changing the word 'fum' to rhyme with each part: 'Fee fie foe *fears*, oh here they are, here are _____'s ears!', or 'Fee fie foe *farm*, oh here it is, here's _____'s arm!'

Learning the names of different body parts is fun and will help your child connect new words with their meaning.

RESEARCH SAYS...

Children whose parents use a wide variety of nouns, adjectives and verbs during conversation with them from birth to age 2 years end up with better vocabularies and higher verbal IQ scores.

♪ where do these go?

from 18 months

This singing game will enhance your toddler's logical thinking skills and boost his vocabulary.

- Play this game when you are helping your toddler get dressed in the morning, during the day, or at bedtime.

- Give your child a choice. Say 'Here are your socks. I wonder where these go?' Sing to the tune of *Do You Know the Muffin Man*: 'Do these go on your ears or feet, your ears or feet, your ears or feet?' Praise your toddler for the right answer.

- Ask similar questions, by singing, as you help your child put on each item of clothing.

RESEARCH SAYS...

'Children aged 4 and 5 years were taught the names of body parts through instructional songs with movements. After 20 days' teaching, their vocabulary and creativity scores were substantially higher than those of children taught by either verbal instruction, or verbal instruction with movements.'

♪ simple simon says
from 2 years

Accelerate the development of your child's creativity and language abilities with this singing and action game.

- Stand in front of your toddler and give instructions to the tune of *Baa, Baa, Black Sheep*, as follows: 'Simple Simon (Sally) says wave your arm like this, wave your arm like this, wave your arm like this!' Show your child how to wave one arm and encourage him to sing.

- Continue with further commands such as kick your leg, nod your head, march up and down, each time acting out your words for your child to copy.

- Later, switch roles so that your child gives the orders and you follow them.

♪ stanley the statue
from 2 years

Singing commands will help your child learn vocabulary related to body parts very rapidly.

- Tell your child that you are Stanley (Stella) the statue. Stand very still and explain that statues don't move.

- Say 'I can't move, but see if you can do what I tell you. Listen very carefully. Are you ready?'

- Sing to the tune of *The Wheels on The Bus*: 'Stanley (Stella) the statue says touch your ears, touch your ears, touch your ears!' See if your child can follow this command. If not, show him how.

- Continue by singing commands to touch other body parts, being careful not to move yourself. Encourage your child to join in with the singing.

what colour?

from 18 months

This choosing game will help your child learn colour names and improve her observation and thinking skills.

RESEARCH SAYS...

'Categorization – grouping things by their similarities and differences – is one of the main ways children learn new words.'

- Draw your child's attention to the colours of everyday objects as you encounter them: a red block, a blue shirt, a yellow banana, a green leaf, a brown teapot.

- Then, focus her attention on the colours of various body parts and items of clothing.

- Ask her questions such as 'These are my teeth (point to them); what colour are they?' If she is unable to answer, give her a choice of two – 'Green or white?'

- Continue in this way with other body parts, then move on to clothing: 'On your hands you have some mittens. What colour are they? Pink or blue?'

same or different?

from 18 months

This game teaches your toddler the concepts of 'same' and 'different', while reinforcing her knowledge of the names of body parts.

- Collect a few of your child's favourite toy animals in a basket and cover with a cloth.

- Now point to your ear and ask 'What's this? This is my _____?' Encourage your toddler to answer.

- Ask her to choose a toy. Then ask 'Is (teddy, say) the *same* as I am – does he have an ear?' Emphasize the word 'same'.

- Have your toddler locate one of teddy's ears, then exclaim 'So teddy *is* the same as I am. He *does* have an ear!'

- Continue in this way with other body parts and toys.

one or two?

from 2 years

Help your child to develop an understanding of the numbers 'one' and 'two', while reinforcing her vocabulary.

- Ask your child 'How many hands do you have? One or two?'

- Then help her count her hands: 'One... two!' Ask her how many hands you have: 'One or two?' Again, help her count.

- Mix up your questions so that sometimes the answer is 'one' and sometimes 'two'. For example: 'How many necks do you have, one or two?'

- Later, draw attention to the body parts of animals. Ask silly questions to challenge her thinking, for example: 'How many wings do you have, one or two?'

what can you do?

from 2 years

- Point to your child's eyes and ask 'What can you do with these? Can you blink them?'

- Now ask your child to point to some part of your body and ask you 'What can you do with that?' If she points to an arm, for example, you might answer 'With my arm, I can wave.' Then wave your arm.

- Next, point to your child's feet and ask 'What can you do with these?' You may need to encourage her by saying 'What are they? Can you jump with your feet?'

- Your child then points to another part of your body and asks 'What can you do with that?' Continue taking turns in this way.

Give your child an opportunity to take charge and make decisions. It will boost her creative thinking as well.

head, arms & legs

from 2 years

Designed to help improve your child's vocabulary, this game also boosts her creative thinking.

- Ask your child 'What can you do with your head? I can shake my head from side to side (shake your head). What can you do with your head?' Encourage her to show you something different she can do with her head and help her describe what she is doing.

- Then ask 'Can you do something else with your head? I can stretch my head way back like this. Can you think of something different you can do with your head?'

- Continue to take turns until neither of you can think of anything else you can do with your head. Move on to your arms, and then your legs.

A A nose & toes
from 2 years

- Face your child and ask 'Can you do what I do?'

- Use both hands to touch your nose, asking 'Can you touch your nose?' Praise your toddler when she copies you.

- Now ask 'Can you touch your toes?' Use both hands to touch your toes.

- Say 'Good! Now can you touch your nose and then toes?' Touch your nose first, then your toes, for your child to copy.

- Move on to other pairs of body parts. Speak quite slowly to begin with.

- When your child becomes good at this, graduate to three body parts. For example: 'Can you touch your tummy, knees and toes?'

RESEARCH SAYS...

In one study, babies whose parents followed a programme of early activities designed to stimulate language development began to say their first words between 7 and 9 months of age. By 10 months, some were uttering simple sentences.

This game will enhance your toddler's co-ordination and balance, and her ability to remember what she hears.

things I do

games to teach your child about daily routines

book projects

from 18 months

Reading books to your toddler and talking about them together will have a significant impact on her many developing abilities.

- Try to read to your toddler every day. Books with lift-up flaps or other features that invite her interaction are ideal. Books about mother and baby, everyday activities, animals or with a repetitive storyline appeal to children of this age.

- Try to include sound effects and strange voices in your reading.

- After reading a book, suggest that you both look back through it to find various people, animals or objects: 'Let's look again to find that monkey (cake, baby, bottle, crocodile, puppy...).' Exclaim in triumph as each search is successful. Encourage your child to suggest things she wants to look for.

- As each is found, repeat the name several times and remind your child what is happening in the picture.

RESEARCH SAYS...

'As soon as a toddler can say about 50 words, her vocabulary begins to explode. On average, this milestone is reached around 18 months.'

shopping

from 2 years

This game helps your child learn about a sequence of events, as well as words that signal the passing of time.

- Pretending to put on your coat, sing to the tune of *London Bridge is Falling Down*: 'Let's go and do the shopping now, shopping now, shopping now, Let's go and do the shopping now, my fair (child's name) – oh!'

- Repeat this pattern of words, with changes to words and actions:

- 'First we find a shopping cart (x3), my fair...' (Collect a wagon, basket or bag.)
  'Now we put the goodies in (x3), my fair...'
  'Next we go to the checkout tills (x3), my fair...'
  'We get some bags and load them up (x3), my fair...'
  'Then we take the groceries home (x3), my fair...'
  'Now we put the food away (x3), my fair...'
  'We've finished all the shopping now (x3), Well done! _____ – oh!'

sorting sorties

from 18 months

Sorting games will improve your toddler's vocabulary, as well as her visual and verbal memory.

- Encourage your child to help you sort clothes into piles (socks, underwear, tops, towels...), or into the appropriate drawers and cupboards, or into groups according to which family member they belong to.

- Together, sort toys into containers or locations. Sort cutlery into compartmentalized trays; sort laundry for the washing machine into white, light-coloured and dark-coloured piles.

- Encourage your toddler to help you sort shoes or socks into pairs and crayons or balls by colour.

♫ good morning!
from 18 months

- Ask your child 'What do we do in the morning?'

- Then sing this song to the tune of *Mary Had a Little Lamb*, encouraging her to join in with the words and actions: 'In the morning, we wake up and stretch, wake up and stretch, wake up and stretch! In the morning we wake up and stretch. Oh, yes we do.' (Lie down, open eyes, yawn and stretch.)

- Ask your child what happens next and then sing another verse based on this. For example: 'We go to the bathroom and wash our faces; we look for our clothes and put them on; we go to the kitchen and eat some breakfast; we go to the bathroom and brush our teeth.' Match the words to your toddler's morning routine.

This game will help develop your toddler's understanding of how events are sequenced in time.

A A 1, 2, 3, feed me!
from 18 months

Mealtimes provide a perfect opportunity to develop your toddler's number concepts.

- Cut up your child's food into bite-sized pieces and help her count them.

- Say 'Oh look, it's some banana! How many pieces? Let's count!' Hold her hand, help her point, and count together: 'One! Two!'

- Ask again how many pieces, and count again. Then count each piece as your toddler eats them.

- Start this game by offering just one, two or three pieces each time. Gradually introduce four, five and six.

concept matching

from 18 months

- **Size** Encourage your child to find pictures of animals or objects in books that are different sizes: large ('big, huge, gigantic, giant-sized'), average ('middle-sized'), and small ('little, tiny, minute'). Use the same terms to describe items encountered in real life. Plastic cups and spoons, cooking pots with lids and painted wooden Russian dolls are useful for this.

- **Colours** Play a book game where you say 'There is something green (blue, red, yellow...) on this page. Can you find it?' Also use colour words to describe things during the day: useful toys include building blocks, stacking cups and crayons.

Help your toddler develop concepts of size and colour by matching what she sees in books with everyday objects.

RESEARCH SAYS...

A toddler of 18 months may say only 50 or so words, but she will understand three or four times as many. Between the ages of 2 and 6 years, children learn the meaning of an amazing eight new words per day!

artist at work
from 18 months

Drawing and painting are excellent ways to boost your child's vocabulary, fine motor skills and creative talents.

- Provide your toddler with suitable drawing and painting materials, different-coloured papers and perhaps a black- or whiteboard.

- Use her random artistic ventures to develop her language skills. Comment and ask questions about the colours, shapes, patterns, and drawing or painting techniques she uses.

- Help your child count the colours she used in her picture, or the number of times she drew wavy, curved or straight lines.

- Compare some of the shapes she produces to known objects: 'That round circle looks like someone's head (a ball, plate, apple...).'

RESEARCH SAYS...

'The amount of language a child hears makes a tremendous difference to her vocabulary and verbal IQ, but it is the quantity of words addressed *directly to her* that is critical.'

hello & goodbye
from 18 months

This game helps develop your toddler's vocabulary and knowledge of routines and social conventions.

- When friends or relatives come to the door, encourage your toddler to greet them, or to say hello in response to their greetings. When they leave, show her how to wave or kiss them goodbye.

- Play a game where one of you goes outside and knocks on the door. The 'visitor' can pretend to be someone well known to the family or a complete stranger. The visitor and the person answering the door then introduce themselves and say hello. Invite the visitor in for a short activity that you and your child act out – this might be sharing a cup of tea, repairing something in the house or playing with toys together.

- Soon the visitor decides to leave, returns to the door and says 'Goodbye (see you again, see you later...).'

telephone talk
from 2 years

This make-believe game develops your child's language skills and concepts about time.

- Give your child a telephone of her own (a toy one, or a spare real one).

- Each day, make her telephone 'ring' and say 'Oh! Your telephone is ringing! It must be your friend _____.' Then talk to your child on your own telephone, in the same room but with a visual barrier between you.

- Disguise your voice and pretend to be the friend who is calling. Ask your child about her day, then finish by suggesting that you talk again tomorrow. The next day play the game again.

let's take turns

from 18 months

- **Snacks** Place a bowl of bite-sized pieces of fruit, cheese, cereal or biscuit between you and your child. Say 'One for you (giving your child a piece), and one for me?' (asking your child for one); 'Now, one for you,' and so on, until all the snacks are eaten.

- **Shopping** At the supermarket, point out different sections of the shop to your toddler, then take turns choosing which section to select groceries from next. Point out when it's 'my turn' or 'your turn'.

This activity reinforces ideas about taking turns and following rules when playing games.

fancy dress

from 2 years

Helping your child dress herself encourages self-confidence and a sense of achievement, but in this game language skills are also enhanced.

- Together, collect some interesting old clothes in a box or old suitcase and check that your child knows the name of each article.

- Ask her to close her eyes and choose an item. Keeping her eyes closed, see if she can guess what it is.

- If she guesses correctly, let her put it on. If she can't guess, let her choose another piece of clothing until she is successful.

- Now it is your turn to close your eyes and guess what item of clothing you have chosen. Your toddler lets you put it on if you guess correctly.

- Continue taking turns. You could both end up in some odd outfits – three hats, one shoe and so on.

cooking exploits

from 18 months

- Invite your child to help you bake a cake, biscuits, small pizzas, a pie, or even homemade modelling dough.

- Let her see you reading the recipe. Have her help to measure out and name the ingredients, pour them into the bowl or wash berries for a pie.

- Describe in detail to your child everything that happens.

- Give her a turn to whisk, mash and mix ingredients, crack eggs and sift flour.

- She can help sprinkle sugar on pie crusts, put raisin faces on biscuits or use her own selection of ingredients to build a mini pizza.

- Explain how long she will have to wait for the dish to cook in the oven, showing her how the clock will look when the time is up.

Young children love to be involved in a baking project. It will enhance language and fine motor skills as well.

RESEARCH SAYS...

Toddlers don't recognize that they are separate little people until the second half of their second year, when some may pass the 'mirror test'. First, a child looks in a mirror. Next, away from the mirror, a dab of paint is put on her face. Back in front of the mirror, she may recognize the change and try to wipe off the paint.

choices

from 18 months

- During everyday activities, offer your toddler choices as often as possible: 'Would you like to wear your white shirt or your blue shirt? Play outside or inside?'

- Your 2-year-old will enjoy this choosing game: fill a small bag with a favourite snack such as raisins or small biscuits and put two large mugs upside down between you. Tell your child you are going to hide a snack under one of the mugs, so she should close her eyes.

- Your child must then guess which mug is hiding the snack. If she is correct, reward her by giving her the snack. If not, repeat the game.

- Later on, switch roles. Your child hides the snack while you guess which mug it is under.

A child of this age enjoys making choices and it helps to build both her vocabulary and her ability to think logically.

bedtime

from 2 years

Toddlers absolutely love the bedtime routine. This game will enhance your child's concept formation and language abilities.

- At any time during the day, play the bedtime game. Choose a favourite stuffed toy, then together put the toy to bed.

- Make the bedtime routine as elaborate as you like and use a few props: a toy baby's bottle, towel, blanket, pillow, book and so on.

- Play other versions of this game where your toddler puts you to bed or you put her to bed.

looking after my friend
from 2 years

- Place items at separate 'daily routine stations' around a room, as follows: a favourite stuffed toy put 'to bed' with a blanket and pillow; some clothing for this toy; a breakfast snack in a bowl; a toothbrush; some toys to play with; a lunch snack on a plate; a washcloth; and finally, by the door, an outdoor object or toy (tricycle, ball, baby stroller).

- Now say 'Oh look, your friend (teddy) has come for a visit. Time to help him get up.' Show your toddler how to help teddy get up and make his bed.

- Follow with visits to get teddy dressed, eat breakfast, brush teeth, play with toys, eat lunch, wash hands and face, and finally, to the door to go out to play.

Daily routines make children feel secure. This game involves acting out some of these, building language and intellectual abilities.

RESEARCH SAYS...

There is no three-word stage in language development. Toddlers remain for several months in the two-word phase while their vocabularies build. Then, early in the third year, they begin to string four or more words together.

in & out of the bath

from 18 months

Bathtimes provide an excellent opportunity for learning about opposites.

- Before your child gets into or out of the bath, ask her 'Is it time to climb *in* the bath or *out*?' Emphasize the words 'in' and 'out'.

- Once she is in, say 'You are *in* the bath.' Now point out other things that are also in the bath and have your child name them.

- Lift objects out of the water and explain 'Now the sponge (boat, soap, cup...) is *out* of the bath!' Ask your child to take other items out and name them – and those that remain in the bath.

- Use bathtimes to demonstrate other opposites such as big and small, cold and hot, wet and dry, shiny and dull.

RESEARCH SAYS...

'Parents direct more negative statements and prohibitions towards boys, and fathers issue more commands to sons. As a result, by age 4 as many as 36 per cent of boys' utterances to each other are either direct imperatives or prohibitions, versus 12 per cent for girls.'

dinner delicacies
from 18 months

Games involving make believe boost your child's imagination and memory, plus her ability to use language.

- Prepare a pretend dinner in a sandbox. You will need plastic crockery and some utensils. Supply wet (water), dry (sand) and solid (small blocks) cooking ingredients.

- Ask your toddler what she would like to cook for dinner and then take turns 'cooking' parts of it. Your child might pour the 'peas' into the saucepan, you add water, she puts it on the 'stove' to cook, and so on.

- Each time one of you completes a step in the 'cooking' process, ask your child what needs to happen next.

what to wear?
from 2 years

This game is designed to accelerate verbal reasoning and logical thinking skills.

- On four cards, draw simple weather pictures: bright yellow sun; dark grey clouds and raindrops; a snowman and snowflake dots; a pale yellow sun and clouds.

- Prepare four piles of clothing to match these weather conditions: a bathing suit and sunglasses; an umbrella and boots; mittens, hat and scarf; a pullover.

- Show your child one of the pictures and ask her to choose the right pile of clothes for that kind of weather. Have her dress up in these items and, together, act out appropriate sunny, rainy, snowy or cloudy weather activities. Then show her another picture and continue the game in the same way.

fun at home

easy activities and naming games around the house

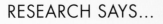

rainbow treasure hunt
from 18 months

Toddlers really enjoy searching games – this one helps to teach your child colour names as well as how to count.

- Say to your toddler 'Let's go on a treasure hunt! Shall we see how many colourful things we can find?' Give him a bag to collect things in.

- Ask him 'What colour should we look for first?' Then find small objects around the house of different colours in turn: a red apple, a green sock, an orange crayon and so on.

- Each time an object is found, compare its colour to a known object: 'This bright blue colour is the same as your T-shirt, isn't it?'

- At the end, together count how many different-coloured objects were found.

- Give your toddler some 'treasure', matching this to the number of colours found (six corn flakes, seven crayons, eight raspberries...).

RESEARCH SAYS...

Parents who consistently respond in positive, encouraging tones to their children's speech and behaviour tend to raise more verbally gifted children.

soup pot
from 2 years

Playing this game
is an excellent
way to enhance
your child's verbal
memory.

- You will need a large saucepan with lid, a large wooden spoon and a basket of small objects. Say 'Let's make soup!' and have your child remove the lid of the pan.

- Ask 'What do you think we should have in our soup?' Let him choose an object from the basket, tell you what it is and place it in the saucepan.

- Then it's your turn. Say 'I think we should put some socks in the soup!' When there are three ingredients in the soup, ask your child to stir it and put on the lid.

- Scratch your head and ask 'Now, what is in our soup? Can you remember what delicious things are in it?' See if he can recall the ingredients.

find the room
from 2 years

A good way to
enhance your
child's visual-
spatial memory
and vocabulary,
this game
combines speech
and movement.

- Walk around the house with your child, saying 'This room is the kitchen, now let's go and find the bathroom.' Locate the bathroom together and then ask 'Can you find the kitchen now?' See if your child can find it. Introduce other rooms in the same way.

- Then spin your child around three times and say 'Perhaps I can muddle your thinking! I expect you won't be able to find the sitting room now!' See if he can locate the correct room. Repeat this for other rooms.

- Later, instead of naming the room, describe it: 'Can you find the room where we cook our food?'

match me up
from 18 months

- Collect pictures of things your toddler can easily find in your house: fruit, toys, furniture or household objects.

- Show your child a picture. Say 'Oh look! Here is a picture of an apple. I know there is a real apple around here somewhere. Can you find it?'

- At first, make the game easier by ensuring that picture and object are in the same room.

- Have your child bring the object to you and compare it to the picture. Discuss together how the pictured and the real objects differ.

Speed up your child's vocabulary development with this pre-reading activity.

poor things!
from 2 years

This game has been designed to improve listening comprehension, and visual and verbal memory.

- While your child is not watching, select a number of familiar items from different rooms.

- Place your collection in front of her and say, 'Oh look! Poor things! This one is a pillow and this is a toothbrush (hold them up for display), but they are not happy! One belongs in the bedroom and one in the bathroom.'

- Ask 'Do you think you might be able to put them where they will be happy again?' Then see if your child can take the pillow to the bedroom and the toothbrush to the bathroom.

- Tell her how clever she is, then return to the pile of items and choose two more.

let me out!

from 2 years

- Collect a set of toys or picture cards to a category in which your child shows a special interest. Put them in a cardboard box and cut a hole in the lid large enough to put a hand through.

- Explain to your child that 'These dinosaurs (vehicles, dogs) want to come out, but they can't unless we can remember their names. Shall we try to help?'

- Take turns to pull out dinosaurs, name them, and describe where they are going. For example: 'Oh! This is diplodocus and he's plodding off to eat plants in this swamp over here.'

- Continue until there are no dinosaurs left in the box. If she has difficulty in remembering a name (make sure you have some difficulty from time to time), the dinosaur is returned to the box and the other player takes a turn.

Play this game when your child is showing an interest in a category of items or animals – such as dinosaurs, vehicles or dogs – to increase her vocabulary rapidly.

RESEARCH SAYS...

When your toddler can say 50–100 words she will be capable of grouping things in categories.

finders, keepers?

from 18 months

- Give your toddler a shopping bag and say 'Let's go and find things!' Then lead her to a room that is not too cluttered with objects.

- Name a small object you think your child might recognize. For example: 'I see an alarm clock! Can you see an alarm clock? The alarm clock is ticking.' Use the name of the object as many times as you can and give hints if necessary to help her find the object.

- Continue to name more objects, extending the search to several rooms. After collecting three or four objects, each player takes a turn to pull one out of the bag and tries to remember where it was found, then returns it to its original location.

Especially appealing to toddlers, this game combines speech and movement. As a bonus, it increases visual memory.

colourful stranger

from 18 months

Teaching your toddler how to classify things according to shape and colour is an excellent way to develop her vocabulary and critical thinking.

- Choose three small toys or objects of the same colour and shape – for example, three red blocks. Show these to your child, explaining that they are all the same colour, and ask 'What colour are they?'

- Now cover the objects with a cloth and slip extra objects of the same type, size or shape but a different colour underneath – for example, a yellow block.

- Have your child remove the cloth, then say 'Oh dear, there's a strange one that doesn't belong with the others. Can you find the one that doesn't belong? The one that is not the same as all the rest?'

air brushing

from 2 years

- On large index cards, draw big shapes with coloured felt pens: a straight vertical line, straight horizontal line, circle, square and triangle.

- Turn your shape cards face down. Invite your child to choose a card and then name or describe the shape.

- Now have your child copy you as you slowly draw the shape in the air with your finger. Take turns practising.

- Then say 'Would you like to try that on paper?' Hold your child's finger gently and help her to draw the shape on a large sheet of paper using her finger.

- Continue with 'Well done! You did that so well! I bet you could draw (paint) a (name the shape) using your crayon (felt pen, paintbrush)!'

- Encourage your toddler to draw as slowly as possible, then as she improves see how quickly she can draw the shape.

RESEARCH SAYS...

While word-learning circuits in the brain begin to mature at 2 years, those responsible for grammatically correct speech do not come into play until the age of 4.

This game is especially good for boys, whose fine motor skills tend to lag behind those of girls.

presents

from 18 months

Learning how to take turns and how to say 'please' and 'thank you' are easily taught in this game.

- Fill a container with small toys or household objects, and sit with your toddler. Say 'Would you like to play a game? This game is called Presents.'

- Explain: 'We need to take *turns*. First, it's your *turn* to have a present. Can you say "Please may I have a present?"' Encourage your toddler to say these words and immediately give him one of the items.

- Say 'Now it's my *turn* to have a present. Please may I have a present?' Have your child give you one of the items.

- Thank your child and name the item: 'Oh! Thank you. It's an eggcup!'

- Have your child copy this by saying 'thank you' and naming the item in his next turn. Emphasize the word 'turn' so that he begins to understand it.

- Continue playing until all the 'presents' are gone.

RESEARCH SAYS...

Language development is greatly accelerated when parents provide lots of positive feedback. Try to confirm, repeat and praise what your child says as much as possible.

sound & seek

from 18 months

Toddlers enjoy imitating animal noises. This game teaches terms used to describe these noises and pairs them with the animals that make them.

- Tell your child you are a duck (or other animal) and you are going to hide. Explain: 'Listen for my quacks. When you hear me quacking, see if you can find me! Don't come until you hear my quacks.' When you have hidden, quack loudly and see if your toddler can find you.

- Then let him choose what animal he would like to be and what noise he will make as a signal for you to find him. Continue to take turns in this way.

- Your toddler will enjoy the game all the more if you have some difficulty finding him and behave as if you are slightly deaf!

alphabet pictures

from 18 months

Your child will love this picture identification game as it provides an opportunity to practise walking and running, as well as to learn new vocabulary.

- Mount an alphabet frieze on the wall at child height. Choose three of the items pictured that you think he might recognize – for example, an apple, a teddy and a cat. Discuss these pictures with your toddler, drawing attention to their colours and various parts.

- Now stand about 1.5m (5ft) away from the frieze with your child and say 'Look at all the pictures!' Ask 'Now where did that apple go? Can you find it?' See if your toddler can run and point to the correct picture. Then ask 'Are you clever enough to find another picture? Where did the picture of the teddy go? Can you find the teddy?'

- Soon your child will be able to find all three pictures easily and you can gradually introduce new ones.

shifty eyes

from 2 years

This game helps your child rapidly translate what his eyes see into sounds or words, and is good preparation for reading.

- Play this game when your child can name colours easily.

- Apply a piece of tape to a tabletop in a long horizontal line. Place two (or three, or four) different-coloured objects side by side on the line at the left-hand end.

- Now have your child 'read' the colours from left to right as fast as he can. For example: 'Green, blue, red!'

- As a reward, allow him to pick up the furthest left object and 'leap-frog' it over the other two, travelling to the right.

- Now encourage him to read this new configuration as fast as he can: 'Blue, red, green!'

- See if he can continue until the three objects reach the end of the line.

- As he improves, add more colours. You could also play this game using shapes or numbers written on cards.

RESEARCH SAYS...

The age at which children begin talking varies widely and cannot be used to predict language skills at school age.

train game
from 18 months

Speed naming of objects, helps to reinforce neural pathways in many regions of a child's brain.

- Place three objects in a row in front of your child. Say 'Look, I've made a train: here's the front, the middle and the end.' Point to the objects from left to right.

- Ask 'What is this part of the train really? And this? And this?' Point to each object and have your toddler identify it. Then ask 'Can you do that faster now?' See if he can name the objects more quickly. Say 'That was excellent! Can you do that even faster now?'

- When he succeeds, exclaim 'Well done! Let's make the train longer.' Add another object to the right-hand end. Ask your child to name the new object and then all four objects as fast as he can, from left to right. Continue in this way and see how long you can make the train.

alphabet trip
from 2 years

Notice how your child's self-esteem and confidence builds as he progresses further with each journey.

- Once your child is adept at Alphabet Pictures (see page 47), stand in front of the frieze at Aa and ask 'Would you like to go on a trip? OK – this is where the journey starts.'

- Then explain that he should name each picture as it appears. He should see how fast he can go and how far he can 'travel' from left to right. When he can no longer name a picture or begins to tire, say 'Well done! You travelled a long way! You named six pictures! So come back 'home' now and I will welcome you with six kisses (treats, hugs). Clever boy!'

- Then play again and see how far he can now 'travel'.

naughty fruit

from 18 months

This vocabulary-building game uses a variety of fruits (or vegetables) and will appeal to your child's desire to handle different objects.

- Help your toddler understand that there are different kinds of fruit. Name and discuss as many of these as you can at home or in the supermarket.

- Place four or five different fruits in a bowl and say 'Look at all the fruit! This one is bright orange. Does it feel a bit bumpy? (let your child handle it) Do you know its name?'

- Discuss the other fruits in the same way. Then, when your toddler is not looking, scatter all the fruits over the table or floor.

- Exclaim 'Oh no! Look at all the NAUGHTY fruit! They hopped out and ran away! We need to call them by name so they come running back!'

- Ask 'Do you know the name of any of those naughty fruit? Yes? Well done! Let's call it by name!' Encourage your child to repeat the name of the fruit with you while he makes it 'scamper' smartly back into the bowl.

- Continue until all the fruit is back in the bowl.

RESEARCH SAYS...

'Encouraging a child to speak himself in response to you enhances language development dramatically. Simple exposure to language on television or radio, or in overheard conversations, does not help a child learn a language.'

who's doing what?

from 2 years

This game utilizes picture books to build your child's ability to understand and use nouns and verbs.

- Collect some simple books that depict animals or people doing different things. Read a book together and talk about the pictures.

- Then say 'Let's find the picture of the pig again. What is he doing?' Repeat the verb (action word) as often as possible: 'Yes, you're right, he is *rolling*. Where is he *rolling*? Does he like *rolling* in the mud?' Continue in this way with other pictures.

- Find books that show more than one person or animal on a page and ask 'Which one is waving? Who is peeping out of the box? Where is the rabbit hiding? What is the dog eating?' These questions will encourage your child to use new nouns (naming words).

squiggles

from 2 years

When your child is accomplished at Alphabet Pictures (see page 47), begin to draw attention to the 'squiggles' in the corner of each picture.

- Stand in front of the first picture together and point to the letter a, saying 'See this funny little squiggle up here? This is an aaa.' Pronounce the sound, not the name. Then say 'What does it say? It tells you that the name of the picture starts with an aaa sound. Can you hear it? Aaa-apple.' Ask him again what it says.

- Now move about 1.5m (5ft) away with your child and say 'Now where did the aaa go? Can you find the funny little squiggle that says aaa?'

- Gradually introduce more letters, being very careful to name them only by their sounds and not by their names.

lost & found
from 2 years

- Find three objects whose names you believe your toddler does not know – for example: a ruler, a cushion and a sponge. Arrange the objects in a row. Talk about each one in turn, naming it several times.

- Say 'Uh-oh! The ruler's wandering off. He's going to get lost!' Carry the ruler off and place it in a bizarre location, but within sight and easy reach for your toddler. Repeat for the cushion and the sponge, placing them in different odd locations.

- Then say 'It's time to find those things now. Can you find the ruler?' Have your child find it and bring it back. Repeat for the other two objects. Now see if he can arrange them in a row in their original sequence.

This game is useful for teaching your toddler three new words at once.

short orders
from 2 years

The purpose of this game is to improve verbal comprehension and memory, but it will also boost your toddler's fine motor skills, co-ordination and balance.

- Write some single-task orders on small pieces of paper, such as: walk backwards, throw the yellow bean bag, climb up and down the stairs, thread two of those curtain rings on to this shoelace.

- Place all the order slips inside a clear jar with a lid. Shake the jar and ask your child to remove the lid and select an order.

- Read it to him and see how quickly he can follow the simple instruction.

- Then let him select another order.

strange menu

from 2 years

- Display 20 or 30 small objects in one corner of the room on a large cloth. Place two plastic bowls (or plates) here as well.

- Seat yourself at a low table and call out 'Waiter! I'm ready to order!' Pretend to be looking at a menu and say 'I would like the pencil, the keys and the soap, please.' Name two (three, four or five) objects that you know are in the 'kitchen' corner.

- Your 'waiter' then has to remember what you ordered, go to the 'kitchen' and find the items. Placing the items in the bowls, he returns carrying something in each hand.

- He places these on the table in front of you, and if he listened carefully you will receive the correct order. Thank him enthusiastically, saying that it looks delicious. If he brings the wrong items, re-order.

This is a game of make believe that has dramatic brain-building effects. If possible, visit a restaurant with your child first, or share a picture book on the topic.

RESEARCH SAYS...

When parents talk to their children they activate the social, emotional and linguistic circuits of their child's brain all at once, but the influence on the developing language systems is the most profound.

let's go

words to discover when you're out and about

twos

from 18 months

- Play this game when out for a walk or in the car.

- Name things as you pass by, saying 'Look! A tree!'

- Ask your toddler to look for another tree and point it out to you. Explain: 'Now we've found *two* trees. I saw a tree and you saw a tree. How many trees have we seen now?'

- Emphasize and repeat the word 'two', and encourage your child to use this word as well.

- Continue to point out and name things that you see, asking your toddler to find a second one.

Teach your child the names of things in his environment and how to count to two with understanding.

the boss

from 2 years

This game will accelerate your toddler's language abilities generally and enhance his verbal memory.

- Explain to your child that you are the 'boss' and he will only get paid if he can follow your orders. Have some 'money' in your pocket in the form of raisins or grapes, then proceed to give one-task orders: 'Run and touch that tree! Ride on the merry-go-round!'

- Each time your child follows the order, exclaim 'Well done!' and give him a piece of 'money'.

- When he can follow one-task orders without difficulty, give him orders with two steps: 'Throw the ball and pick it up again! Sit on the swing and stick out your tongue!' Eventually, your child may be able to follow a three-step order: 'Pick up the ball, bounce it on the ground and sit down!'

travel treasures

from 2 years

- Ask your toddler 'Would you like to travel in search of treasure?' Provide him with a box or backpack as a 'suitcase'.

- Say 'We begin the journey on a jet,' then with arms outstretched, zoom off to a random location in the park, garden or wherever you are.

- Invite your child to look for treasure here. Then say 'I can see a green pebble (red ball, orange leaf).' Have your toddler find this treasure and let him put it in his 'suitcase'.

- Explain 'Now we have to catch a train!' Then shuffle along together making choo-choo noises, until you reach a different 'country'.

- Continue travelling and hunting for treasure. Use different means of transport between locations.

A vocabulary-expanding game, this also provides your child with the opportunity to improve his balance and co-ordination.

RESEARCH SAYS...

When a child hears and uses language it operates to shape the brain circuits that analyse speech sounds, interpret meaning and grammar, and control the ability to speak.

touching encounters

from 18 months

This vocabulary-building game can be played in the car, at the park or beach, out in the countryside, or anywhere there are unbreakable objects that your child can touch.

- If, for example, you are walking in the countryside, you might say 'That tree has interesting-looking bark. Let's see how it feels!'

- Then tell your toddler to close her eyes and feel the bark. Ask questions that give her a choice of answers: 'Does it feel rough or smooth?'

- Feel the bark yourself, saying 'Yes! You are right, it does feel smooth.'

- Then look for other things to touch, and talk about how they feel.

RESEARCH SAYS...

'A child's language development is speeded up when parents' responses are attentive (the parent repeats, confirms or extends what the child says), warm (the parent gives more positive than negative feedback) and encouraging (the parent more often invites or asks than makes direct commands).'

shop talk
from 2 years

This is an easy way to enhance your child's observational and language skills, while you do the shopping!

- The supermarket is a great place to familiarize your toddler with different colours.

- Begin by pointing out the colour of something near you: 'Oh look, some yellow cheese! What else is yellow? Let's look for something else that is yellow.'

- If you see something yellow that your child has missed, point it out to her by asking 'Are those lemons yellow?'

- When you have found two yellow items, move on to a different colour. If your toddler points to an item she is not able to name, identify it for her.

- Then point out another colour and continue the game.

where did we go?
from 2 years

This game teaches vocabulary and concepts related to time. It will also help improve your child's memory and verbal skills.

- Help your child review the day's events by asking 'Where did we go today?' Help her recall what you did first, and discuss the details.

- Ask 'What did we do after that?' If she can't remember, prompt her. For example, say 'We were hungry, weren't we? Where did we go to have lunch?' Jog her memory to remember the details. Then ask 'After that, after lunch, what did we do?'

- When you have discussed all the things you did, review the day by listing in order four or five events. See how many of them your child can list in the correct order.

♫round the mountain
from 18 months

You can play this vocabulary-boosting game at the beach, during a walk in the woods or in the countryside.

● Make up words to sing to the tune of *She'll Be Coming Round the Mountain*. For example: 'He'll be galloping (hopping, tip-toeing, zooming) round the mountain when he comes...'

● Sing the words as you and your child act them out.

● Then make the words more descriptive and as silly as possible: 'He'll be waddling like a duck (leaping like a frog, trotting like a horse when he comes.'

● Later, make the movements even more complex by singing a second verse: 'He'll be patting at his head (blowing his trombone, quacking like a duck, looking right and left) as he gallops (hops, tip-toes, zooms).'

RESEARCH SAYS...

'Language development is critically shaped by experience. The language networks of a child's brain wire up properly and permanently only when exposed to the sounds, meaning and grammar of a human language.'

A A slippery places
from 2 years

In this game, you increase your toddler's verbal abilities by asking silly questions about where you are going.

- When out in the town, ask questions like: 'Does the baker sell bread or fish? Will the dentist look at my knees or my teeth?'

- Later, make the game more challenging by deliberately making ridiculous remarks: 'We need to return to the parking meter to put in some more potatoes.'

- If at first your child does not notice your errors, repeat what you have said and seek agreement from him.

- When your child does notice, tell him how clever he is and how absolutely silly you are.

A A my favourite things
from 2 years

Amuse an older toddler during long journeys or waiting times with this speech sound game.

- Tell your child your name is Sss-simon (Sss-sally), drawing out the beginning sound, and you only like things that sound the same as the beginning of your name – 'things that begin with sss!' Ask 'Can you think of something I would like?'

- Your child asks you 'Would you like (biscuits, ham)?' Each time you shake your head and say 'no'. As soon as he says a word that starts with the sss sound (slugs, sausages...), you say 'Yes! I love sss-slugs!'

- Continue until he has thought of three words that begin with the sss sound and then become a different character, changing your name. Names that start with S, M, F, N, V are best to begin with, as the beginning sounds can be drawn out and emphasized more easily than other letter sounds.

pet detective

from 18 months

- When your toddler is not looking, hide various animal toys around the garden and then say 'I can't find your teddy bear, or your sheep, or your giraffe. I think they must have come outside to play, too.'

- Say 'Maybe they are lost. Shall we look for them?' Stroll around, then say 'Oh! I can see something brown behind that tree. Who is it?'

- See if your child can name the animal as she retrieves it.

- Continue the search for the remaining animals, each time giving your toddler clues about their location.

Playing this hide-and-seek game teaches descriptive vocabulary.

clueless

from 2 years

This game boosts verbal reasoning skills and language development while keeping your child amused during a long wait or car journey.

- Tell your child that your name is Clueless. Your brain doesn't work properly. You can think about things but you can't remember their names. Ask 'Would you like to help me think of the names of things?'

- If you have a son, he will be interested in the properties of objects. Ask him questions like: 'I'm thinking of something that ticks and tells the time (a machine that cleans carpet) – what is it called?'

- If you have a daughter, other people's behaviour will hold more fascination for her. Ask these kind of questions: 'I can't think of the name of the hair on grandpa's chin (what your grandmother wears to help her see better) – what is it called?'

silly milly

from 2 years

- Ask your toddler if she would like to play Silly Milly (Silly Billy).

- Explain 'I will tell you something silly to do, and then you think of something silly for me to do. Are you ready?'

- Then say 'Make your ears wave at me!', or 'Flap your arms like wings!', or 'Purr like a cat!'

- Your toddler follows this command, then it's her turn to give you a silly command.

- If she is unable to think of something that does not require you to move too far from the spot, take another turn yourself until something occurs to her.

This vocabulary-building and creativity-boosting game is ideal for those testing times when you are waiting in a queue.

RESEARCH SAYS...

Parents can help their child's language development by using a variety of words and sentence structures, and by making connections between an unknown word and words she already knows.

postman
from 18 months

Some preliminary preparation is required for this symbol-matching and naming game.

● You will need to establish several 'residences' around the garden (start with three). Using stiff index cards, draw a symbol on each. Begin with simple shapes: circle, square, triangle, rectangle. Attach the cards at various sites at your child's height. These are the 'addresses' of the dwellings.

● Using either real envelopes or index cards, make a set of 'letters'. Address each, in this case, with a shape.

● Give your toddler a bag containing the letters and examine them together, discussing their addresses. Then see if she can deliver the letters to the correct houses by matching the addresses.

● When your toddler knows the names of the shape symbols, vary the game by addressing the letters and labelling the houses with numbers or letters.

RESEARCH SAYS...

'Babies as young as 13–15 months actually notice the grammar and word order in sentences, and use this information to help them understand what is being said.'

nature match
from 18 months

This is an excellent language game to play when you and your toddler are out for a walk.

- Draw your child's attention to an eyecatching leaf (flower, shell, pebble, seed pod...). Talk about its shape, colour and size, then say 'I wonder if we can find another one the same?'

- Help your child find a matching object, then explain that now you have 'two the same' you have a matching 'pair'.

- Then find another object and try to create another matching pair. See how many matching pairs you can find during your walk.

bus, car, jeep, van
from 2 years

This spot-the-object and counting game can be played when you are out walking or in the car.

- Challenge your child to spot different kinds of vehicles. Say 'Let's take turns and see how many different kinds of machines are on the road today!'

- Have your child count on her fingers as different vehicles are spotted: 'Car! That's one!' Show her how to hold on to one finger.

- Next, she may point to and name a bus. Show her how to hold on to two fingers. If your child points to a vehicle she cannot name, tell her what it is and show her how to hold on to another finger.

- Aim to find five different kinds of vehicles, one for each finger of one hand. Gradually increase the target number and have her count fingers on both hands.

slides & swings

from 2 years

- Give a description of one piece of equipment: 'It's something silver that has a ladder and a chute you can slide down; it's something to sit on that swings back and forth.' See if your child can locate it quickly, run over to it and tell you its name.

- If she succeeds, praise her and tell her that as a reward, she may play on the slide (swing, rope ladder...) for two minutes. Time this, then give her another description.

- Each time your child locates and names the equipment correctly, let her play on it for a minute or two as a reward. If she has difficulty, describe another piece of equipment and see if she can locate and name that one.

Help your child learn the names of the equipment in a playground by repeating them often, as she plays on each one. Then play this game.

jungle safari

from 2 years

Play this game outside in a place where there are some trees and low shrubs. It will teach your child verbal comprehension, verbal memory and listening skills.

- Tell your child that you will count to 20 and as soon as you reach 20 she should stop moving. During this time she must find a place to hide.

- Tell her: 'I'm going to stay here and pretend to be a big lion. When I stop counting it means I am asleep.' Continue with: 'Try to sneak up for a closer look at me. But watch out! If I hear any noise I will wake up and try to see you!'

- Count to 20, close your eyes and listen for noises. See how close your child can get to you without being seen. Take turns to be the lion and the person on safari.

obstacle race

from 2 years

- Set up an obstacle course for your toddler: a 'valley' (cardboard box) to climb in and out of, a 'huge mountain' (upturned laundry basket) to circumnavigate, a large 'lake' (green or blue tablecloth or blanket) to swim across, some 'stepping stones' (cushions or paper plates) to negotiate, and so on.

- At first, keep the obstacles to a minimum. As your child improves, gradually increase the number.

- Show her the target destination, where the enticing prize or refreshment awaits. Show her where to start the 'race' and announce 'Ready! Set! Go!'

- Help her negotiate the course, and as she progresses talk about each obstacle, naming it repeatedly.

- Later, vary the game by timing the race and challenge her to name each obstacle before negotiating it.

This game boosts many varied skills including visual and verbal memory, vocabulary, co-ordination, balance and creativity.

RESEARCH SAYS...

Children spoken to most by their parents during the first 3 years of life end up with superior reading, spelling, speaking and listening abilities 5 years later.

what's that sound?

helping your toddler
recognize familiar noises

high & low
from 18 months

- Walk around the house together and point to various objects, asking 'What's that?' Encourage your toddler to identify the object by name.

- Then ask 'Can you tell me what this is called in a tiny, little, high voice like this?' Demonstrate how to say the word in a high voice and encourage her to copy you.

- Point to another object for your toddler to name and then ask 'Can you tell me its name in a big, deep, low voice like this?' Demonstrate how to say the word in a very low voice and encourage her to copy you.

- Continue in this way, having your child name things in either a high or a low voice.

This game trains your toddler's ability to hear high- and low-pitched voices.

bus trip
from 2 years

Singing songs together will help your child to concentrate on the sounds heard in speech, which is important when learning to read and spell.

- Teach your child *The Wheels on The Bus* song: 'The wheels on the bus go round and round (repeat 'round and round' three times), The wheels on the bus go round and round all through the town.'

- Then: the horn on the bus goes beep, beep, beep; the doors... go open and shut; the wipers... go swish, swish, swish; the people... go up and down; the baby... goes 'Waah, waah, waaa'; the bell... goes ding, ding, ding. Sing this song and act out the words together.

- Adapt the words to other forms of transport: the wheels on the train go clickety-clack....

I'm a little teapot
from 2 years

- Teach your toddler the song and actions for *I'm a Little Teapot*: 'I'm a little teapot short and stout, Here's my handle and here's my spout, When I get all steamed up then I shout, Tip me over and pour me out.'

- When your child knows this song well, talk about the sounds made by other objects around the house. Using the same tune, change the words and actions to suit the object. For example: 'I'm a little telephone quiet for a while, Here's my handle and here's my dial, When someone telephones then I sing, Pick me up and stop the ring.'

- Discuss the sounds made by a clock, kitchen kettle, sprinkler or jack-in-the-box toy, and make up words and actions for these objects.

This singing activity helps to develop vocabulary and listening skills.

RESEARCH SAYS...

One auditory ability that is rather poor in young children is sound discrimination in a noisy setting. When they are learning the subtleties of speech, it is best if background noise can be kept to a minimum.

who's talking?

from 18 months

Children are fascinated by animal noises. This game helps your child learn the vocabulary used to describe these sounds.

- Show your child two stuffed toy animals – for example, a dog and a sheep – and make each animal 'talk'.

- Say 'Oh! Listen! Here's the dog! The dog is saying woof, woof, woof! And here is the sheep. The sheep says baa, baa, baa.'

- Ask your toddler to close her eyes and listen. Then make one of the animal noises and ask 'Who is talking? Is it the dog or the sheep?'

- Help your child to guess which one, or demonstrate again what each animal 'says'.

- Gradually introduce more animals and animal noises for your toddler to identify.

RESEARCH SAYS...

'**From 3 to 6 months, a baby's ability to hear high-pitched sounds begins to develop; by 7 years, children can hear the highest tones better than adults. The ability to hear low-pitched sounds, however, matures much more slowly, improving very gradually until a child reaches puberty.**'

soft & loud
from 2 years

This game involves trying to imitate the sounds heard in the environment, an activity that demands close attention.

- Listen for sounds together at home, in the car, or while out and about. Try to imitate the noises heard, asking your child 'Can you make that noise?'

- Then say 'I can't hear you. I'm a bit deaf. Can you make the sound very loudly, please?' Encourage your child to make the noise loudly.

- Then say 'Oh! I have very sensitive ears! Can you make that sound very quietly, please?' Then see if your child can make the sound very quietly.

- Ask her to say things to you in a big, loud voice and in a tiny, quiet voice, and teach her how to have conversations where you both whisper.

what makes this noise?
from 2 years

Once your child is used to playing Soft & Loud (see above) and can identify sounds in the environment, try making up your own for her to listen to.

- Make some sounds and see if your child can identify what would make them.

- If you give her a choice of answers, she will find this a lot easier.

- You might say 'Hoo, hoo: is that the wind blowing or the thunder booming?' or 'Tick, tick, tick: is that water dripping or a clock ticking?' or 'Ding-dong, Ding-dong: is that the noise of jingle bells or a door bell?'

sound detectives

from 18 months

Enhance your toddler's ability to concentrate and distinguish particular sounds from everyday background noise.

- Sit down with your toddler and ask 'Can you hear any noises in this room?'

- Help him locate the source of any sounds he hears and identify what made them. Then say 'Listen carefully. Can you hear any sounds coming from the next room (kitchen, bathroom, outdoors...)?'

- Each time, go and locate the source of the noise and identify what made it.

- Then, in this new location, listen together for more sounds to identify.

- Each time you play, begin the game in a different room.

RESEARCH SAYS...

'Babies grow steadily quicker and more precise at locating sounds during their first 6 months. This ability then continues to improve very gradually, until a child is about 7 years old.'

weather sounds

from 2 years

While enhancing language development, this game also helps to improve your child's ability to concentrate and listen carefully.

- When out for a walk or in the car, ask your child 'What kind of day is it today? How does it sound?'

- Ask other questions to draw his attention to the sounds that accompany different conditions: 'Can you hear the raindrops pitter-pattering on the roof? Why are the buses and trees making so much noise today?'

- Talk about the sounds made by feet crunching on frost, swishing through leaves or squelching in wet mud. Discuss how wet days sound different to dry ones – car tyres on wet roads or puddles splashing.

- Tell your child to close his eyes and see if he can guess what kind of day it is, just by listening.

surrounding sounds

from 2 years

Develop your child's ability to identify where sounds are coming from.

- Go for a walk with your child and find a place to sit down together. Then say 'Let's see what sounds we can hear.' Have your child close his eyes to improve his concentration. Ask 'Can you hear a sound yet?'

- When he hears a specific sound, tell him to keep his eyes closed and point to where it was coming from.

- With eyes open, together follow the direction in which he is pointing and see how accurate his ears were. Say 'Let's follow the direction and get closer. Is this the right direction? Shall we get even closer?' Take turns to listen and point. Sometimes the direction might be straight up, in which case simply look up.

fast talk, slow talk

from 18 months

Combining speech and movement is one of the best ways to boost language and listening skills.

- Demonstrate various movements – marching, jumping, running, spinning, bending, waving, wiggling – and teach your child the name of each one.

- As you march around the room or outdoors, say 'Let's march! March, march, march...' Encourage your toddler to copy you while saying the word 'march' in time to her movements.

- After a short time, suggest another movement: 'Let's sway! Sway, sway, sway...' Again, have your child copy your movements and join you in saying the word 'sway'.

- At first, say the words and move in time to them very slowly. Later, alternate 'fast talk' with 'slow talk', so that sometimes you and your toddler talk and move very slowly and sometimes very quickly.

RESEARCH SAYS...

Children who have difficulty discriminating sounds that change within fractions of a second are likely to have problems using and understanding speech. This ability improves in children between the ages of 3 years and puberty.

transporting sounds
from 2 years

This game teaches vocabulary associated with vehicle noises and helps boost listening skills.

● Display pictures of various vehicles and/or toy vehicles, in a row so that your toddler can see them easily. Talk about the noise each vehicle makes and have your child copy the noises.

● Then say 'Now are you ready to play a special game? Listen very carefully. Your ears must be very clever.' Explain: 'I am going to make a noise. See if you can find the picture or the toy that goes with that sound.'

● Make various vehicle sounds, helping your child to find a picture or toy vehicle that makes that sound.

● Start with three or four pictures or toys and gradually increase the number.

find the noisy one
from 2 years

Your child will enjoy this auditory and visual memory game.

● Collect some household objects or toys that make a noise, such as a bell, a rattle, or toy animals.

● Show the objects to your child, letting her make noises with each one. Discuss the noises as she does this. Then ask her to close her eyes while you use one of the objects to make a noise.

● After you have made the sound, tell your child to open her eyes and guess which object made the noise. Ask 'Which was the noisy one?'

● Take turns being the listener and the sound-maker.

who am I?

from 2 years

- Crawl around quickly, barking like a dog, and ask 'Who am I? Am I a dog or a rabbit?' Wiggle along on the floor saying 'Sss, sss, sss' and ask 'Who am I? Am I a lion or a snake?'

- Act out other animals, and gradually make your questions more difficult: 'Am I a snake or a lizard?' When your child is expert at this, take turns to act out animals for the other player to guess.

In this auditory and visual memory game you pretend to be an animal and ask your child to guess who you are.

farm animals

from 2 years

An excellent all-round brain-booster, in this game your child listens for the sounds of farmyard animals and has to identify them.

- Look at picture books about farm animals with your child and make all the animal noises together. Or, teach your child to sing *Old Macdonald Had a Farm*.

- Ask him if he would like to be the farmer. Then tell him to stay in the corner of the 'field' (this can be indoors) until he hears one of the hungry farm animals calling.

- Now scamper off somewhere and hide. Pretend to be a cow (pig, horse, duck...) and call out loudly and repeatedly with the appropriate animal noise.

- Your child, the 'farmer', then comes to tend you. She will need to identify what animal you are in order to feed you your favourite food.

- Later, take turns to hide.

fine tuning

AA

from 2 years

- Show your child two different toy vehicles that have different-sounding wheels, or two different whistles, or rattles. Demonstrate how each makes a different sound.

- Now say 'I bet I can guess which one is making a noise without looking.' Put your hands over your eyes.

- Instruct your child to make a noise with one of the objects. You might say 'Oh dear! I can't guess which one that is. Can you make its noise again?' Identify the object by describing its details: 'It's the blue plastic whistle' (not the paper whistle that rolls out).

- Let your child take a turn hiding his eyes and guessing which object you make a noise with. Later, increase the number of objects to three.

This is a more challenging listening game, which requires your child to discriminate between two similar sounds.

RESEARCH SAYS...

Be particularly vigilant for symptoms of ear infections in your young child, since even very subtle changes in his early auditory experience can affect language development.

first songs
& rhymes

enjoying simple tunes and finger games

flying by

from 18 months

You can expand this finger game into more verses by introducing different insects – but always keep the final verse the same.

- 'Here's a honey-bee, He sits on your arm, He walks a little, But he means no harm.' (Fingers land on your toddler's arm, then 'walk' up and down a little very gently.)

- 'Now here's a fly, He lands in your hair, He buzzes about, But you don't care!' (Fingers land softly on your child's hair and move about a little, making bzzz, bzzz noises.)

- 'Here's a mosquito, He thinks YOU taste right, Watch out for him! He wants a BITE! (Fingers zoom in, as you make high-pitched eee! eee! noises, and try to land on parts of your child's body; your other hand helps your child to bat the 'mosquito' away.)

RESEARCH SAYS ...

'Early childhood musical (or rhythm and rhyme) experiences, especially if they involve the parents, are one of the most powerful ways to accelerate the "wiring up" of a child's brain.'

AA ten little bunnies
from 18 months

This is a good finger-play game for enhancing your toddler's number and vocabulary skills.

- 'Ten little bunnies hop out one day' (All ten fingers 'hop'.)

- 'To dig some holes' (All ten fingers 'dig' holes.)

- 'And to play and play' (All ten fingers scamper around.)

- 'Five have a nibble' (Fingers of one hand 'nibble'.)

- 'Five fall asleep' (The other fingers lie flat and still.)

- 'Then along comes a fox' (Your face looms in closer.)

- 'And... watch them LEAP!' (All fingers on each hand 'leap' off in opposite directions.)

AA four birdies & a cat
from 18 months

This finger-play will help to develop your toddler's counting skills.

- 'One little birdie twittering at you' (wiggle one finger.) 'Another one says "How do you do?"' (Hold up a finger on the other hand and make it 'talk' to the first finger.)

- 'Two little birdies twittering at you' (Hold up two fingers on the first hand, wiggling them a little.) 'Another one says "Let's coo and coo!"' (Hold up one finger on the other hand and make it 'talk' to the first two fingers.)

- Repeat the words and actions for the third finger, using the reply 'Another one says "Can I do it too?"' Holding up the fourth finger, reply 'Along comes a cat and he says... "Boo!"' (Hold up your thumb and make it 'pounce' on the other fingers, which all disappear quickly.)

♫ nursery rhymes
from 18 months

- Teach your toddler some simple nursery rhymes. Buy books, tapes and CDs that you can enjoy together, reciting and acting out the rhymes. Now change the words to make them more personal to your child. Try to include her name whenever possible.

- For example: 'Pat-a-cake, pat-a-cake, baker's man, Bake me a cake as fast as you can, Pat it and prick it and mark it with a T (C, B, D, G, P, V – if your child's name begins with one of these letters), And put it in the oven for (your child's name) and me.'

- Or, 'Hickory, dickory dock! (your child's name) ran up the clock, The clock struck one and _____ ran down, Hickory, dickory dock!'

Including your child's name in the words of familiar nursery rhymes will delight her.

AA to & fro in the snow
from 18 months

Your toddler will have fun reciting and acting out this rhyme in winter.

- If it is snowing outside or you have been reading a book about snow, recite this action rhyme together:

- 'Snow, snow, falls without a sound.' (Hold your arms up then lower them while making your fingers 'dance'.)

- 'Let's make an angel. Lie on the ground.' (Lie on the floor and move your arms up and down to make 'wings' in the 'snow'.)

- 'Snow, snow, look how softly it falls.' (As first action.)

- 'Uh-oh! Watch out for my snowballs!' (Pretend to 'throw' your snowballs.)

fun in the sun

from 18 months

- Draw your child's attention to the sunny day outside, then recite this rhyme in a slow, steady rhythm:

- 'Sun, sun, shining so bright' (Hold your arms over your head and bring them slowly down to form a big circle.)

- 'Let's swim, swim, out of sight' (Pretend to swim.)

- 'Sun, sun, shining so light' (Repeat first action.)

- 'Makes a swim feel just right!' (Pretend to swim.)

- Encourage your toddler to join in with your words and actions.

This rhyme will help your toddler develop concepts about weather conditions.

RESEARCH SAYS ...

Music stimulates all the senses, training your child's brain to organize and conduct numerous activities all at the same time.

A A cakes

from 18 months

Encouraging your toddler to copy these words and relatively complex actions will help improve his verbal memory, comprehension and fine motor skills.

- 'A little cake' (Make a fist.)

- 'A larger cake' (Cover your fist with your other hand.)

- 'A great big cake I see!' (Open out your hands, fingertips touching to make an even bigger ball shape.)

- 'Now let's count the cakes we made, One! Two! Three!' (Repeat the actions in sequence.)

- Change the words and actions for a 'hedgehog' (bear, lion) verse, starting as curled-up balls on the floor and making your bodies grow progressively bigger.

RESEARCH SAYS ...

'Being exposed to speech is the most important form of stimulation a child's developing brain receives.'

A A this is the way
from 18 months

This is a traditional rhyme with a surprise ending that children love. Your toddler will pay very close attention to the words as a way of preparing himself.

- Place your child on your knees facing you and hold his hands. Then recite the rhyme:

- 'This is the way the gentleman rides – trit-trot, trit-trot, trit-trot.' (Alternate knees rise and fall at a sedate pace.)

- 'This is the way the lady rides – can-ter, can-ter, can-ter.' (Knees rock at a slightly faster pace.)

- 'This is the way the old man rides – hide-ee-hee, hide-ee-hee, hide-ee-hee. And – down into the ditch!' (Knee movements are jerky and slow, then tip your child gently off your knees.)

A A one to five
from 18 months

Performing this finger-play is an excellent way to introduce your toddler to early counting skills.

- Hold up your thumb: 'One, one, one, that's a thumb.'

- Hold up two fingers and say 'Two, two, two, eyes of blue.' (Gently touch each eye with each finger.)

- Three fingers: 'Three, three, three – all having tea.' (Draw the tips of the three fingers together.)

- Four fingers: 'Four, four, four – look at them roar!' (Flash the fingers up and down.)

- Now, hold up all five fingers, spread out, and say 'Five, five, five – let's take a dive!' (Align the fingers side by side and, like a diver, take your hand up, bend the fingers and swoop down into a steep 'dive'.)

♫ simple songs
from 18 months

- Songs where the words can be easily accompanied by actions are fun. When your toddler knows some, use familiar tunes to introduce new words.

- For example, describe what you or your toddler are doing by singing new words to the tune of *Row, Row, Row Your Boat*: 'Ride, ride, ride in the car (on the bus, on your 'trike', in the stroller, on mummy's knee, on daddy's shoulders...), Gently down the street, Merrily, merrily, merrily, merrily, I wonder who we'll meet?'

- The meaning might often end up a little ridiculous: 'Hide, hide, hide (wash, munch, play, sing, clap...) in the bin (sink, tree, bush, tub, box...), Gently for awhile, Merrily, merrily, merrily, merrily, This is just my style!'

Learning the words to simple songs is an excellent way to develop your child's language abilities.

♫ singing toys
from 18 months

This singing game will expand your toddler's knowledge and understanding of action words.

- Arrange animal toys or puppets around the room. Then sing this song to the tune of *Rock-A-Bye Baby*. 'My name is (Teddy), I like to play, Tell me your name, Please tell me, okay?' Have teddy approach another toy and pretend to be singing to it.

- The toy that was approached sings in return: 'My name is (Bunny), I like to play, "Bunny" is my name, But I'm (hopping) today.'

- Bunny hops off to the next animal and repeats the first words that teddy sang. Continue like this, moving each animal in a different way.

fast planes & slow trains

from 18 months

- Sing this song to the tune of *Row, Row, Row Your Boat* and perform the actions:

- 'Fly, fly, fly your plane, Wherever you want to go, Merrily, merrily, merrily, We can go fast and slow.'

- Sing the song very slowly once or twice while you both fly (arms outstretched) around the room slowly. Then sing the song faster several times, zooming around much more quickly.

- Further verses could include: 'Drive, drive, drive your car; Paddle, paddle, paddle the canoe; Ride, ride, ride your horse', and so on. You can make this game all the more interesting for your toddler by supplying props, such as an improvised steering wheel.

Repetitive action songs are an excellent way to develop language, balance and timing.

RESEARCH SAYS ...

After participating in a programme involving music, movement and drama, disadvantaged children's self-esteem scores were significantly higher.

♫ let's bop

from 18 months

Many pop songs have catchy tunes and simple, repetitious words and rhythms that will boost your toddler's memory and enhance her awareness of rhythm and rhyme.

- Play some pop music for your toddler. Pick her up and dance together, or allow her to dance on your feet.

- Sing along to any songs you know and praise her when she joins in.

- Later, sing one of the songs unaccompanied and encourage her to join in.

- Give her a simple instrument such as a mouth organ or rattle and see if she can play it in time to the music.

- Take turns playing different instruments to various songs, encouraging your toddler to hum or sing along.

RESEARCH SAYS ...

'Between 2 and 3 years, learning to hear the beat or rhythm in a song helps develop abilities that underlie learning to read and spell. However, parents may not be making the most of this time: studies show that only 10 per cent of kindergarten children are able to keep a steady beat.'

one little chicken
from 18 months

Teaching your toddler the words and actions to this finger-play will have dramatic effects on her language, memory and fine motor skills.

- 'One little chicken, pecking at a crumb' (One finger 'pecks' at the table.) 'Another one says "Can I have some?"' (One finger on the other hand 'talks' to the first one.)

- 'Two little chickens pecking at a crumb' (Two fingers 'peck'.) 'Another one says "I'm your chum!"' (One finger on the other hand 'talks' to the first two fingers.)

- Repeat for the third finger, using the reply 'Another one says "I need to fill MY tummy-tum-tum!"'

- 'Four little chickens pecking at a crumb' (Four fingers 'peck' at the table.) 'Along comes a fox and he says – 'YUM!"' (The other hand 'bites' at the 'chickens'.)

follow the leader
from 2 years

This language- and memory-boosting game also promotes co-ordination and balance.

- Ask your child to stand behind you and try to copy what you do. Then start tip-toeing (marching, sliding...) or walk while arm-waving or clapping.

- Sing to the tune of *Twinkle, Twinkle, Little Star*: 'Twinkle, twinkle, do you see? Can you, can you, copy me?' Sing this several times, checking that she is copying you.

- Now ask your toddler to be the leader. Have her repeat the movements and sing a second verse several times: 'Twinkle, twinkle, I could see, Clever, clever, clever me!' Now you follow, copying her movements. Then you become the leader, sing the first verse again and invent a new way of moving for your toddler to copy.

rain refrain

from 18 months

This is a good action rhyme to perform together when it is too wet to play outdoors.

- Draw your toddler's attention to the rain outside.

- Recite the following rhyme in a slow, steady rhythm while performing the actions:

- 'The rain, the rain is pouring down.' (Reach each arm alternately up and down in front of you.)

- 'Puddles to jump in – but don't drown!' (Pretend to jump and fall in puddles.)

- 'The rain, the rain, is soaking our hair.' (Repeat the first action, but also pretend the rain is pouring down over your face.)

- 'But puddles are fun so we don't care!' (Continue to jump in 'puddles'.)

- Encourage your child to copy your actions, and if you repeat the rhyme over and over he will soon learn the words, too.

RESEARCH SAYS...

Preschool children who received training involving musical games and songs gained an IQ advantage of 10–20 points. Ten years later, they had higher reading and maths scores.

A A rhymes on purpose
from 18 months

Playing with the sounds of language appeals to a child's sense of humour, and this activity speeds learning of the logic of grammar.

- Teach your toddler the well-known rhyme 'To market to market, to buy a fat pig, home again, home again, jiggety-jig.'

- Then, whenever you are on an outing you can adapt it to tell your toddler what is happening. Encourage him to recite with you and maintain the rhyming part.

- 'To market, to market, to buy some dinner (bread, eggs, bananas), Home again, home again, jiggety-jinner (jed, jegs, jananas).'

- 'To the checkout, the checkout, to pay some money, Home again, home again, jiggety-junny.'

♫ rainbow song
from 2 years

This song will develop your child's memory, vocabulary and overall intelligence.

- First, teach your child to sing the well-known song *Baa, Baa, Black Sheep*.

- When he is familiar with the tune, teach him to sing these words to it: 'Red, orange, yellow, green, Blue and in-di-go, Vio–let! vio–let!, Don't forget!'

- Whenever you spot a rainbow in the sky, discuss the colours with your child and sing the song together.

- Paint rainbows together, discussing how to make the colours, or see if your toddler can arrange different-coloured crayons in the correct rainbow order.

tongue twisters
from 2 years

- Following the same pattern as *Fuzzy-Wuzzy was a Bear*, make up new rhymes:

- 'Slippy-Slimy was a snake, But Slippy-Slimy had no lake, So Slippy-Slimy wasn't slippy, slimy – was she?'

- 'Canny-Danny is a train, But Canny-Danny has no brain, So Canny-Danny cannot be canny Danny – can he?'

- Based on *How Much Wood Could a Woodchuck Chuck*:

- 'How many crocs would a crocodile dial, If a crocodile could dial crocs?'

Young children love to play with the sounds of language and these tongue twisters provide an early challenge.

letter-sound songs
from 2 years

When you have played Squiggles (see page 51) and your child can pronounce the *sound* of a letter in reponse to seeing its shape, play this game.

- Point to one of the lower-case letters on an alphabet frieze or in a book that your toddler can recognize and encourage her to join in as you sing to the tune of *Mary Had a Little Lamb*:

- 'This is the squiggle that says a-a-a, a-a-a, a-a-a, This is the squiggle that says a-a-a, A-a, a, A, a-a. Sing the letter *sound*, not the letter name. Repeat for other letters your child can recognize.

- Your child may begin to recognize lower-case letter shapes on signs, cereal boxes or in magazines. Join in with him as he sings the appropriate letter-sound song.

♫ find the letter

from 2 years

- Sing this song whenever there is an opportunity to draw your toddler's attention to a letter shape and sound with which he is familiar. Focusing on lower-case (rather than upper-case) letter shapes is far more useful for learning to read.

- Sing to the tune of *Mary Had a Little Lamb*: 'I can see a mm – mm – mm, a mm – mm – mm, a mm – mm – mm, It's somewhere on this page (box, wall, floor, door).'

- Then sing: 'Can you find the mm – mm – mm...? It's somewhere on this page.'

- See if your child can find the letter. Remember to use only letter *sounds* – knowing letter *names* causes some children substantial confusion later when learning to read.

This is an excellent game to teach your child the shapes of letters and their sounds – the most important factor in predicting reading ability.

RESEARCH SAYS...

A group of 3-year-olds were given 50 minutes a day of singing lessons while another group received piano lessons. After nine months, both groups showed amazing improvement in their ability to put together a puzzle, a way of measuring mathematical reasoning skill.

making music

musical fun using everyday household objects

jingle bells
from 2 years

- Gather some metal bracelets, keys, coins and blunt metal bolts. You will also need two clear jars with lids and some string.

- Help your child thread the string through the bracelets and tie them loosely together, then let him shake them.

- Ask him to fill a jar with the coins and close the lid. Now let him shake the jar and listen to the sound it makes.

- Help him to make more instruments by stringing the keys together and filling the jar with metal bolts.

- Let your child jingle one of his instruments in time to music. See if he can play and dance at the same time.

Making simple musical instruments to play can provide your child with hours of enjoyment. Only play this game if he has stopped putting things in his mouth.

pat-a-cake tambourin
from 2 years

Your child's self-esteem is enhanced when he makes his own musical toy to play in time to music.

- Help your child make a tambourine from two paper plates, string, and about ten jingly items.

- Punch four or five 1cm (¼in) holes evenly around the rim of each plate. Put the plates together to create a space inside, matching up the holes. Thread string through each pair of holes, tying loosely.

- Let him select two jingly items, then tie them together using the string at each pair of holes. Show him how to hold the tambourine with one hand and tap it with the other. See if he can play the tambourine in time to the rhyme 'Pat-a-cake, pat-a-cake, baker's man...'.

kitchen symphony
from 18 months

- Gather different-sized saucepans, some with lids, bowls and utensils such as a large metal spoon, a whisk and a wooden spoon.

- Play some classical music and show your toddler how to beat an upturned saucepan or saucepan with lid in time to it.

- Put some dried pasta, whole walnuts or coins into a ceramic bowl or saucepan. Your child can stir this to make a tinkling sound in time to the music.

- Bang two saucepan lids together at dramatic points in the music. Allow your child to experiment with this new instrument.

- Allow him to create his own 'symphony' by playing the different instruments in time to the classical music.

When you are working in the kitchen, these ideas will keep your toddler happy and improve his reasoning skills.

RESEARCH SAYS...

Musical activities that focus on rhythm skills, such as tapping out the beat of a song while singing, can improve spelling ability later on.

soft shoe shuffle

from 18 months

- Give your toddler two large, empty matchboxes and show her how to rub the rough sides gently together to make an interesting sound.

- Together, sing one of her favourite songs and encourage her to rub the matchboxes together in time to the rhythm. Discuss what the sound reminds her of: 'Does it sound like scuffling feet? Or shuffling slippers?'

- Have her copy you as you take shuffling steps and listen together to how this sounds.

- Now sing her favourite song again, while she plays the matchboxes in time to it and takes shuffling steps.

Help your child to make a simple instrument using matchboxes.

let's sing about it

from 2 years

Helping your child to compose her own lyrics develops her imagination and creativity.

- Choose a repetitious tune your child knows well and ask her to suggest words to describe what is happening at the time. Then say 'Those are good words!' and ask 'Would you like to sing about that?' Accompany your song with the most convenient noises or 'instrument'.

- For example, to the tune of *The Wheels on The Bus* you might sing: 'The peas in my mouth are popping and popping... Now I'm chewing and chewing my chicken...' and so on. (Here, the 'instruments' are eating noises.) If you are out, you might sing: 'Now we are driving and driving along...' and so on. (Clapping hands or tapping feet could be your 'instruments'.)

♫ performer

from 2 years

- If there is a song your toddler can sing by herself, ask her to sing it while you record this on a childproof tape recorder.

- Show your child how to rewind the tape. Then say 'Let's listen to your performance now!' Show her how to press the 'play' button.

- Tell her how much you enjoyed her singing and encourage her to sing the song again, either faster or slower.

- Help her rewind, playback and listen.

- Encourage your child to sing and record other songs.

This activity helps to improve your child's self-esteem, persistence, fine motor skills, and maths- and reading-related abilities.

RESEARCH SAYS...

First-year pupils were taught folk songs with an emphasis on melody and rhythm. At the end of the year, and a year later, their reading scores were substantially higher than those of children who did not receive this instruction.

♫ tubular tootings

from 18 months

Making simple instruments is a good way to introduce your child to their different names.

● Collect some different-sized cardboard tubes. Say 'Look! We have some horns to blow!'

● Let your toddler hold each one and hum or 'toot' a tune as he pretends to play. Show him how different wind instruments are held – 'This is a flute' (holding a tube horizontally out to one side); 'This is a clarinet' (tube held vertically); 'And this is a trumpet' (tube held straight out in front).

● Say 'Let's play our flutes (clarinets, trumpets)!' Have him copy your placement of the instrument and finger actions. Toot or hum melodies together.

● Produce interesting noises: tie some plastic wrap tightly over the tops of your 'horns', place your lips lightly against it and blow. The sounds will vary, depending on the sizes of your tubes.

RESEARCH SAYS...

'In one brain imaging study, musicians who began their musical training before the age of 7 were found to have brains that differed noticeably in structure compared to non-musicians. The part of the brain that links the two halves of the brain was larger in musicians.'

hey diddle, diddle
from 18 months

If you accompany familiar nursery rhymes with actions, your child's attention is automatically secured.

- Teach your toddler the nursery rhyme *Hey Diddle, Diddle*, and talk about the illustrations to it in a book.

- Act out the rhyme by pretending to play a 'fiddle', then jumping 'over the moon', then laughing like the 'little dog' and then running away hand in hand.

- Now make some 'instruments'. Place an elastic band around a cereal box to hold a wooden spoon on it, the handle extending off one end. Use another wooden spoon as the 'bow' for this 'fiddle'. Use a plastic plate and another spoon as a drum and drumstick.

- Now sing the rhyme together – one of you 'plays' your new fiddle while the other beats the 'drum'.

drums for all
from 2 years

Encouraging your child to play a drum in time to music enhances automatic balance and motor co-ordination, a prerequisite to tackling more complex tasks.

- Help your toddler make a snare drum from a cardboard egg carton and some string. Give him two paintbrushes as drumsticks. Hang the drum around his neck so that it rests horizontally against his tummy. Then hum or play some band-type music and march together as he beats his drum in time to it.

- Using a cardboard hat box or plastic laundry basket, help him create a 'jungle' drum. Then hum or play some jungle music, and have your toddler sit cross-legged on the ground and play the drum with a wooden spoon.

- You can make drums for pop or symphony concerts.

♫ water music
from 18 months

- Collect plastic bottles of different sizes and shapes, with lids screwed on loosely.

- Fill a large plastic tub with water. Then see if your toddler can unscrew the lids and fill the bottles with different amounts of water.

- Help him screw the lids on again tightly, then listen to the sounds made by shaking the different bottles.

- Now play some music on tape or CD. Choose a bottle each and shake it in time to the music.

- See if he can play two water shakers at once, and accompany both fast and slow music in time to the beat.

You may not stay very dry during this activity, but it will yield benefits for your child's analytical thinking.

♫ spicy music
from 2 years

Your child will be intrigued by the wide variety of sounds that can be produced by changing the contents of a jar.

- Collect some clear herb/spice jars with lids. These are ideal for tiny hands. Help your child fill each jar with a different noise-maker – beans, peppercorns, rice, lentils. Tighten the lids and listen to the sound each makes.

- Ask your child to place three 'shakers' in a row. Tell him to close his eyes and listen to each one in turn. Then shake one of the three and see if he can guess which one it was. Let him test your listening abilities in a similar way.

- Have him choose his favourite shaker and play it in time to different kinds of music.

♫ musical chairs
from 2 years

- Make a circle with small cushions or chairs and place a musical instrument (toy or homemade) on each one.

- Ask your child to choose an instrument, then show him how to walk around the circle playing it.

- Say 'Well done! Can you do that in time to this music?' Then play some music on tape or CD.

- After a minute, turn off the music and say 'You are so good at that! This time, listen for when the music stops and see if you can stop, too! Remember – as soon as it stops, stop walking and stop playing. Are you ready?'

- Give him several practices at this. Eventually, tell him that he stopped brilliantly.

- Tell him he can exchange his instrument for a new one – the one on the nearest cushion or chair.

- Continue the game in this way.

This game is a great opportunity for your toddler to play an instrument in time to music.

RESEARCH SAYS...

Evidence suggests that playing music enhances brain development more than just listening to it.

♫ parade
from 18 months

Playing an instrument while moving is a complex task for young children and stimulates the neural circuits in many regions of the brain.

- Collect toy band instruments that are light enough to carry around – bells, shakers, trumpet-shaped party whistles or horns, or homemade drums.

- Say to your toddler 'Let's go on a parade!' Then each choose an instrument.

- Play some band-type music with a pronounced beat and march around together, playing your instruments in time to it.

- Then change instruments and play again, or change the music and see if your toddler can keep time to this.

RESEARCH SAYS...

Music-making stimulates the development of neural pathways in the brain that are involved in reasoning, creative thinking, decision-making and problem-solving.

swell bells

from 2 years

This problem-solving activity is ideal for budding scientists.

- Set out three tall glasses (with sturdy bases) in a row. Help your child to make a bell-like noise by striking (not too hard!) one of the glasses with a metal teaspoon.

- Help her discover that the edge, not the bottom of the spoon, sounds best. A loose grip also gives a clearer sound. If the glass is struck near the rim, not the base, the sound is more bell-like.

- Adjust the water level in each glass so that she can produce a low 'daddy' sound, a middle 'mummy' sound and a high 'baby' sound.

- Make up different 'songs' by varying the order and the number of times she strikes each 'bell'.

comb & tissue tickle

from 2 years

This activity is an especially useful way to improve reasoning and fine motor skills.

- Show your child how to make a simple 'mouth organ' with tissue paper and a plastic comb.

- Fold the paper around the comb and ask her to put the instrument in her mouth and blow gently. Ask how her lips feel when she blows: 'Do they tickle?'

- Take turns playing music for each other, replacing the tissue paper. While one person plays, the other dances a 'tickly' dance on tiptoes in time to the music.

- Vary the speed and rhythm of the music, so that your child performs different dances on tiptoes.

matchbox magic
from 2 years

- Fill the matchboxes with tiny biscuits, currants or sultanas.

- Help your child make two or three shakers. Then sing favourite songs and nursery rhymes, and see if she can shake her shaker in time to them.

- Then see if she can dance around in a circle while singing and playing her shaker at the same time.

Small matchboxes make ideal shakers. Make sure that the contents are safe for toddlers to eat.

snippity-snap
from 2 years

Ballpoint pens with clicking tops make excellent pretend instruments and are useful tools for accelerating fine-motor skills.

- Find two pens like this and show your child how to make a clicking sound.

- Say 'Can you do this?' Make two clicks with your pen and congratulate her ability to copy you.

- Gradually challenge her to copy more and more complex click sequences.

- Your child may also enjoy giving you sequences to copy – occasionally make errors to see if your child notices.

- Think of things that make clicking sounds and then sing to the tune of *The Wheels on The Bus*: 'The switch on the lamp goes snippity-snap, snippity-snap, snippity-snap...; The wheels on the train go clickety-clack...'. See if your child can make the right sequence of clicks to the words 'snippity-snap (clickety-clack)' – three quick ones followed by a slow one.

♫ rattlesnake
from 2 years

- Acquaint your child with the concept of a rattlesnake. You could look at picture books or visit the zoo.

- Say 'Let's be rattlesnakes! We need to make some rattling tails.' Help your toddler tie rustling or jingling objects with pipe cleaners to a length of coloured chenille (or string) at intervals. Use small bells, curtain rings, pieces of foil or small matchboxes filled with peppercorns.

- Teach your toddler this song to the tune of *I'm a Little Teapot*: 'I'm a little rattlesnake, Long and thin, Here is my rattle, And here is my grin; When I get excited, I make a din! Here comes my bite! Sharp like a pin!'

- Pin your tails to your trousers or skirt and perform actions in time to your singing: wiggle and squirm along the ground, hold up your rattle and shake it, display a large grin, shake your rattlesnake tail again, and bare your fangs (teeth) and pretend to bite, chasing after each other.

RESEARCH SAYS...

Singing lessons and group music play have been shown to boost the creative thinking and motor skills of 3- and 4-year-olds.'

This make-believe game will increase your child's overall intellectual and creative talents.

music all around

listening and responding
to all types of music

♫ ready, steady
from 18 months

- During day-to-day activities, play music on a sound system or tape recorder, so that your toddler begins to associate an activity with a particular kind of music.

- During any of these sessions, clap your hands, tap your toes, shake a rattle or play an instrument in time to the music that is playing.

- Encourage your child to join in. See how long he can keep a steady beat. He may find this easier with particular kinds of music.

- Try alternating claps, where you clap your own hands and then each other's. Attempt to maintain a steady beat throughout.

This activity is designed to improve your toddler's overall brain functioning.

♫ all kinds of music
from 18 months

By exposing your child to a wide variety of music, you stimulate regions of the brain responsible for spatial, verbal, balance, memory and other skills.

- Play different kinds of music for your toddler. Let him respond in whatever way he chooses – by dancing, singing, humming, or playing with his toys more calmly or with more concentration than before.

- Try to expose him to classical music, pop, jazz, opera, nursery rhymes, country and western, marching tunes, and Asian music. Watch his reactions and you will soon learn what kind of music he prefers.

- Tell him the name of his favourite composer (song, band, album, type of music). He may request it by name. Be sure to praise his excellent memory.

same or different?

from 2 years

- Sit with your back to your child and say 'I am going to make two noises.' Then make two identical sounds (whistles, coughs, claps, clicks, squeaks, kisses) separated by a few seconds. Ask 'Those two noises were the *same*, weren't they? Listen again. Can you tell me if these two noises are the *same*?'

- Make two new identical noises, asking 'Were those two noises the *same*? Did they sound the *same*?' When your child understands, tell him how clever he is.

- Now make two varying noises. See if your child can tell that they were *different*. If not, show him how you made the noises, so he can see that you had to do something different to produce each one.

- Continue making noises that are the *same* or *different*, encouraging your child to use these words.

Your child's ability to discriminate sounds will be improved by playing this game.

RESEARCH SAYS...

Listening to music has physical effects on the body that can affect a child's emotional state, stress and activity levels, and his sensitivity towards others. In one study, the presence of background music increased the number of social interactions among children.

♫ if you're happy

from 18 months

This singing activity is an excellent way to expand your toddler's vocabulary, as the possibilities for lyrics are almost endless.

- Young children love the song *If You're Happy and You Know It*.

- Sing the first part, substituting different words: 'If you're happy (sleepy, hungry, cross, tiny, huge, thirsty, washing, sneezing, an airplane, a bus, a train...) and you know it...' Then stop and ask 'What are you going to do?'

- See if your toddler can suggest an action to perform, then sing this version of the song together, performing the new actions.

- If he is unable to suggest anything, ask questions like: 'Should we go and lie down? Nibble on this biscuit? Have a hug?'

- You could also help give him ideas by singing alternate verses, where you sing responses such as: 'When I'm warm and friendly I give you a kiss (hug, cuddle); When I'm hot and bothered I wash my face (go and lie down, wave my arms); When I'm curious about something I ask questions (read a book, scratch my head...)'

RESEARCH SAYS...

Music instruction that includes listening, visual and motor activities can improve reading ability.

♫ sharp ears
from 2 years

This listening game helps build your child's auditory discrimination skill, as well as his thinking and reasoning abilities.

- Sit your child in a large, comfortable chair. Go behind the chair and ask him to listen carefully. Explain that you are going to 'play' two pieces of music. Say 'But sometimes it is very difficult for me to think of two pieces of music that are not just the same. Here are two pieces of music. Listen to see if they are the *same* or *different*.'

- Continue with 'Here's the first music', then clap once. 'And here's the second music', then clap twice. Ask 'Were they the *same*? Was the second music the *same* as the first music?'

- Begin with very simple rhythms and your child will soon be able to make high-level listening decisions!

♫ DJ dancer
from 2 years

By giving your child some control over the music he wants to listen to, you enhance his self-esteem, listening and critical thinking skills.

- Let your child have control over the station dial on a radio. Challenge him to find some music he likes. When he does, dance together in time to the beat.

- Then, let him find another station with music he likes. Clap together in time to the beat.

- For the next piece of music he finds, hum along together in accompaniment. For the next piece, sway to the music without moving your feet.

- You can also play this game by showing your toddler how to select different tracks on a CD.

♫ copycat
from 18 months

- Sit facing your toddler and say 'Your ears are looking pretty sharp today. I bet they can hear anything! Shall we make some music together? Can you do this?'

- Then clap a very simple rhythm – perhaps two claps separated by a few seconds.

- Then ask 'Can you do that?' Gradually make the series of claps more complex – two slow claps followed by three quick claps, four quick claps followed by two slow ones, and so on.

- Encourage your child to copy you, repeating any rhythms that need more practice. Give plenty of praise for good copying.

This is another auditory discrimination and memory game.

♫ beat that!
from 2 years

This game is targeted at improving your child's auditory memory, which is fundamental to virtually all learning.

- Show your child a toy (or homemade) drum or tambourine and let her play randomly with it. Then ask 'Would you like to play what I play?'

- Tap out a simple rhythm for your toddler to listen to.

- Ask 'Can you play that?' See if your child can copy the rhythm you made, giving her help and praise.

- Start with very simple rhythms – perhaps just two taps. Then try two quick taps followed by one slow tap, and so on. Eventually your toddler might create simple rhythms for you to copy.

♫ one, two or three?

from 2 years

- Sit your toddler beside you in front of a keyboard instrument (toy or real). Play one note and ask your child to play one. Then ask 'How many notes did I play? How many notes did you play?' Praise your child if she answers correctly both times. Otherwise, repeat the exercise.

- Then ask 'Shall we play two notes now?' Then play any two notes. Encourage your child to copy you by playing any two notes.

- Ask 'How many notes did you play that time? And how many did I play?' Act very pleased if she answers 'Two!' Teach the concept of 'three' in the same way and then play this game.

- Say to your toddler 'Close your eyes. How many notes can your ears hear?

- Then play one, two or three notes. Ask your child to open her eyes and tell you how many notes she heard: 'One, two or three?'

Research reveals that early keyboard instruction – the focus of this game – enhances brain development in a variety of ways.

RESEARCH SAYS...

Musical instruction can improve both reading and maths skills. After underperforming primary school students were given musical instruction, they caught up with average pupils in reading and were ahead in maths.

♫ where has it gone?

from 2 years

This singing game will improve your child's visual memory.

● Put three small objects (sock, comb, toy car, teaspoon, toothbrush, eggcup) on a large plastic plate or tray and show them to your toddler. Ask her to name each object and if she does not know one, name it for her.

● Through discussion, ensure that she says the name of each object herself at least twice. Ask her to close her eyes and name the three objects. Then say 'Please wait there while I take this away for a minute' and carry the plate away. Out of view, remove one of the items.

● Return and say 'I'm afraid I was so hungry I've taken one of the things away to eat! Do you know which one?'

● Take turns testing each other. On returning with the plate, the player sings to the tune of *Oh Where, Oh Where Has My Little Dog Gone?*: 'Oh dear! Oh dear! Which one is gone? I wonder which one it can be...?'

RESEARCH SAYS...

'In boys, the left side of the brain seems to handle the lyrics of a song while the right side is more involved in remembering melody. In girls, both sides of the brain tend to be involved in both these processes.'

♫ do you know the name?

from 2 years

One-on-one conversations are the best way to accelerate your toddler's language development.

- To the tune of *Do You Know the Muffin Man*, sing to your child 'Do you know the name of this, the name of this, the name of this?... (repeat)... Tell me if you can.'

- Point to a body part or an object. Or, to elicit a verb from your child, act out something such as combing hair, brushing teeth or driving a vehicle.

- Help her sing in response: 'Oh yes I know the name of that, the name of that, the name of that... (repeat)... That is called a _____ (That is known as _____).'

rhyming games

from 2 years

Finger-plays can be adapted to become rhyming action games that will help to develop your child's sense of rhythm, rhyme, balance and tempo.

- You and your child can make up games together, but here are some suggestions to get you started.

- 'Round and round the racing track... (run around in a large circle side by side with your toddler) Like a racing car, One zoom, two zooms... (take two large, lunging jumps) And look where we are! (dive to the ground crashing into one another).'

- 'Round and round the garden... (prance around together in large circles) Like a tabby cat, One step, two steps... (stop and take two prancing steps) And a pounce like that! (pounce on your child as if catching a mouse).'

♫ keyboard copy
from 2 years

- Place your toddler beside you in front of a piano, electric keyboard or organ (toy or real). Say 'Look at your clever little fingers. Are they ready to play?' Let her experiment, pressing the keys as she likes.

- Then say 'Let's play a game! Do you think you can do what I do?' Play one note on the keyboard and see if your child can play that same note.

- Next, play two notes that are side by side on the keyboard. Use the same finger for each note. See if your toddler can copy you. Progress to three notes, all of them side by side, using one finger only. Later, show her how to use more than one finger, progressing to three notes (three fingers) or more.

A musical keyboard activity helps to develop the spatial reasoning abilities that underlie maths and science.

♫ who came first?
from 2 years

This game helps improve your child's ability to discriminate pitch.

- Hold up your little finger and say 'This is Little. This is the sound he makes.' Then hum a very high note. Hold up your thumb and say 'This is Big. Here is the sound he makes.' Then hum a very low note.

- Now say 'Oh! Big and Little both want to talk,' and hum a high note followed by a low note. Ask 'Who came first – Big or Little?' If necessary, repeat the notes.

- Then say 'Oh! Big and Little both want to talk again,' and this time hum the low note followed by the very high one. Ask again 'Who came first?' Continue with other pairs of high and low notes.

dressing the part

from 2 years

- Gather some props for you and your child to use when listening to different kinds of music.

- Dress in cowboy hats and boots, play some country and western music, and dance in that style – hands on hips and clap your hands.

- Dress in shoes that are too large and some silly hats; make your noses red. Play some circus music and behave like clowns – do somersaults and pull hats over each other's eyes. Try to move in time to the music.

- Dress formally in bow ties, play some classical music and let your child take part in a 'concert', playing along in time to the music on a keyboard instrument (toy or real).

Make-believe and fantasy games like this accelerate the development of many cognitive abilities.

RESEARCH SAYS...

Three-year-olds given piano keyboard training developed spatial abilities that were 34 per cent better than another group of children who had been trained for the same amount of time in computer keyboard skills.

♫ mood music

from 2 years

Encouraging children to respond to music can improve vocabulary, emotional and motor abilities.

- Gather a selection of music to encourage different emotional responses from your child, for example: happy, sad, grumpy, sleepy or silly.

- Play some happy-sounding music and say to your child 'Does this music sound happy? Does it make you feel like smiling?' Then smile at each other. Ask 'Does it make you feel like dancing?' Then dance together.

- After a few minutes, play some sad-sounding music and ask 'How does this music sound to you? It doesn't sound so happy, does it? Does it make you feel sad?' Make sad faces at each other.

- Ask 'Does it make you feel like crying?' Pretend to weep, wiping your eyes. Continue the game in this way.

RESEARCH SAYS...

'Children as young as 3 years are good at detecting the emotional mood of a piece of music. They can match happy or sad cartoon faces with various kinds of music played to them quite accurately.'

leap frog

from 18 months

A child of this age probably enjoys musical activities most when they involve movement, as in this game.

- To the tune of *Mary Had a Little Lamb*, sing 'Little frogs like to leap, leap, leap, leap, leap, leap; Little frogs like to leap, leap, leap; That's what frogs like to do.'

- One player curls up small like a frog and the other player 'leaps' (climbs) over. Then the first player climbs over, and so on. Sing the song together several times.

- Then ask 'What do rabbits do?' 'Leap' as before, while singing: 'Little rabbits like to hop, hop, hop...'. Perform any other 'leaping' verses you can think of.

- Change the actions for 'Little snakes like to slither and slide...', and 'Little birds like to fly, fly, fly...'.

ride a white horse

from 2 years

This singing game is a fun way to speed your child's intellectual development.

- One player is the horse and the other the rider. Dress the horse in a white cloth and attach some 'reins' (a long ribbon around back of the neck and under the arms). Attach bells to the rider's toes and tie rings made of string around one finger of each hand. Attach metal bangles to these rings.

- Horse and rider now gallop off singing *Ride a Cock Horse*: 'Ride a white horse to Banbury Cross, I'm a fine lady upon (gentleman on) a white horse, With rings on my fingers and bells on my toes, I shall have music wherever I go!' Try singing at different speeds, the 'horse' adjusting its actions accordingly.

the hunting trip

A A

from 2 years

- Begin with 'Let's go and hunt bears! Are you ready? OK, put your feet on the road like this and here we go!' (Place one hand on each knee; children copy.) 'Here we go, walk, walk, walk, walking down the road.' (Pat one knee, then the other, in a steady rhythm.)

- Then ask 'What's that ahead?' (Put hand to brow and look puzzled; children copy.) 'Oh! It's a river. Have to swim it! What do we have to do?' (Children repeat and copy your swimming actions.) Then say 'Back on the road again!' (Children repeat and resume knee patting.)

- Carry on like this, encountering 'obstacles' along the way. Finally, having asked what's ahead, you say 'It's a BEAR!' Start 'running' (pat knees much faster) and repeat all the actions rapidly in reverse order, saying: 'Back on the road!' and so on, until 'Home at last!'

This story activity, where children copy your actions, is fun to play with a group.

sing & point

from 2 years

This game combines singing with actions and brings many benefits, both physical and intellectual.

- To the tune of *Oh Where, Oh Where Has My Little Dog Gone?* take turns singing these verses to each other:

- You sing 'Oh where, oh where is mummy's (daddy's) nose (knee, toe...)? Oh, where, oh where, can it be?' Continue singing until your child locates and points to the part of your body you named.

- She then sings 'Oh where, oh where is (her name)'s chin (neck, elbow, thumb...)? Oh, where, oh where, can it be?' You then point to the part of her body that she named. Continue taking turns to sing your questions.

naughty notes

from 2 years

- Play one note in a series on a toy piano, keyboard, xylophone, guitar or other musical instrument.

- Tell your child that all the notes sounded the same because you played the same note each time. Play the sequence again for her to listen to.

- Ask her 'Do all the notes sound the same? Or did a naughty note creep in?'

- Take turns being the 'listener' and the 'player', so that your child will have a chance both to listen and to devise a series of notes for you to listen to.

This odd-one-out game is an excellent way to train auditory skills.

RESEARCH SAYS...

Early experience with songs, sung by loving parents, helps build neural networks in the brain involved with social-emotional development.

index

acknowledgements

PHOTOGRAPHY

Octopus Publishing Group Limited/Adrian Pope 1, 6, 7 Top, 8 top left, 8 top right, 8 Bottom, 10, 17, 18, 23, 24 top left, 29, 30, 35, 36, 38 top left, 38 top right, 38 Bottom, 40, 43, 45, 46, 48, 50, 53, 54 top left, 54 top right, 54 Bottom, 57, 58, 60, 63, 64, 68 top left, 68 top right, 68 Bottom, 71, 72, 74, 76, 79, 80 top left, 80 top right, 80 Bottom, 82, 85, 86, 89, 95, 96 top left, 96 top right, 96 Bottom, 99, 101, 102, 105, 106, 109, 110 top left, 110 top right, 110 Bottom, 113, 114, 117, 118, 121, 122, 125/Peter Pugh-Cook 3, 7 bottom, 13, 14, 20, 24 top right, 26, 33, 67, 90, 92

Executive Editor **Jane McIntosh**
Editor **Charlotte Wilson**
Executive Art Editor **Leigh Jones**
Designer **Ruth Hope**
Production Controller **Manjit Sihra**
Picture Researcher **Luzia Strohmayer**

word and music games

for toddlers and twos